Interaction of Color

JOSEF ALBERS Interaction of Color

50TH ANNIVERSARY EDITION

YALE UNIVERSITY PRESS
New Haven & London

Yale University Press books may be purchased in quantity for educational, business, or promotional use. For information, please e-mail sales.press@yale.edu (U.S. office) or sales@yaleup.co.uk (U.K. office).
yalebooks.com/art

Set in Baskerville type
Original edition designed and set by Norman Ives
4th edition designed and set by BW&A Books, Inc.
Printed in China by 1010 Printing International Limited.
Library of Congress Control Number: 2012953675
ISBN: 978-0-300-17935-4
10 9

Plate XIX-1 (r.): Henri Matisse, *Femme au chapeau* (Woman with a Hat), 1905, oil on canvas, 31 3/4 × 23 1/2 in. (80.65 × 59.69 cm). San Francisco Museum of Modern Art, Bequest of Elise S. Haas. © 2012 Succession H. Matisse, Paris/Artists Rights Society (ARS), New York. Photograph by Ben Blackwell.

This book is my thanks to my students

TABLE OF CONTENTS

FOREWORD

It is now fifty years since *Interaction of Color* was published and, almost immediately, began to change the way people all over the world thought about seeing. Shortly after it came out, it became a best-selling book, as it has been ever since. Its success is easy to understand, for it brings infinite personal pleasure while perpetually expanding the way that colors are used and perceived in art, architecture, textiles, interior design, and graphic media at every level of technology. Yet we should not forget that when it was initially published, *Interaction* was, like everything Josef Albers did, a brave experiment, and like all forays into the unprecedented, it was the subject of controversy.

Even if for the most part *Interaction* was highly praised, occasionally the response was far from laudatory. Writers vary in their responses to negative criticism—some saying it is fine, since all that counts is the amount of coverage, others feeling stung. Josef Albers, who saw himself as something of a martyr to modernism, both regretted the attacks and was intrigued by them. Part of the fascination of being blasted was that it confirmed that he had really startled people and taken them beyond their normal comfort zone. Ever since he had left a world where art was practiced in an acceptable, academic way—in the academies of Berlin and Munich, and in the public education system in which he taught in his native Westphalia—and gone to the Bauhaus, he had known what it was to inspire such controversial response.

Bauhaus modernism may now be in the pantheon of acceptability, but back then it startled and displeased the larger audience. The same was true of Black Mountain College, where Albers went after 1933, when the Bauhaus closed, and where he remained for sixteen years; today that pioneering institution is worshiped, but at the time a lot of what was created there was viewed as a form of heresy. Later, in 1950, when Albers began his *Homages to the Square*, he was mocked. Twenty years after that, when he was the first living artist given a solo retrospective at The Metropolitan Museum of Art, the work that people like Clement Greenberg had lambasted was finally recognized for its ingenuity, integrity, and subsuming beauty. Now that half a century has passed it has achieved the status, however dubious, of being a blue chip financial commodity, but at the start it was, like any statement by a messiah, criticized vociferously.

When Yale University Press courageously, and with all of the superb standards required by as exacting an artist as Albers, brought out *Interaction of Color* in 1963, the publication generally had an easier time than most of the artist's ventures. This was equally true when the paperback version came out in 1971. But there was the occasional diatribe. And Albers, proud as he was of the sales and all the enthusiasm for the book, of the applause worldwide, was fascinated at being a lightning rod for dissent. The octogenarian clipped the few bad reviews that appeared along with dozens of favorable ones and tried to find out more about their authors. The voices of "nay" appeared in obscure publications, but they still counted. One of the reasons the artist was so interested was that the things for which the critics attacked the books were exactly the elements that excited him the most, because they recommended such a radical departure from traditional, hidebound ways of seeing.

Arthur Carp was the author of an attack in the magazine *Leonardo*. To present the flaws, Carp wrote that Albers considered "good teaching . . . 'more a matter of right questions than . . . of right answers.' He deprecates 'self-expression,' as opposed to 'a basic step-by-step learning.' . . . Students are urged to use disliked colors in the hope they may overcome their prejudices." Carp used these points to demonstrate that "one doubts if Albers is really being helpful" and to justify the statement "Would that he were less of a dilettante (pejorative connotation)!"

Everything that Carp attacked, of course, was what Albers believed in and what others applauded. As Howard Sayre Weaver wrote in a review that appeared in 1963 following publication of the first edition, *Interaction of Color* was a "grand passport to perception." It assumed that glorious role because it was, "essentially, a process: a unique means of learning and teaching and experiencing."

Weaver referred to Albers's fondness for the words of John Ruskin: "Hundreds of people can talk, for one who can think. But thousands of people can think, for one who can see." Most people, sooner or later, have recognized the miraculous way in which *Interaction of Color* facilitates such seeing. In the 1963 *Architectural Forum*, a design teacher at Cooper Union was among those prescient enough to write, "*Interaction of Color* is the most comprehensive and intelligent, as well as the handsomest, book we yet have on this subject. It is an indispensable volume for the artist, architect, or teacher who finds a greater challenge in discovery than in a 'safe' color system." That same year, Dore Ashton, reviewing the book in *Studio*, was perceptive enough to recognize that Albers was the opposite of the pedagogue Carp accused him of being; rather, his achievement justified his comment that "teaching is not a matter of method but of heart." The year after the paperback came out, the poet Mark Strand, in *Saturday Review*, saw Josef Albers's work as demonstrating that "when color challenges the safe, enclosing geometrical properties of the pictorial surface, as it is meant to, it does so with a slowness and delicacy that are disarming and a beauty that is exhilarating."

What one person disdained, another saw as groundbreaking. Albers's approach was revolutionary, putting experimentation at the fore. It disputed traditional notions of taste. It sought to engage rather than merely inform.

As a keen observer of the human comedy, Albers was particularly aware that sometimes his detractors were well-known figures, and his champions obscure ones. Donald Judd, in *ARTS Magazine* in 1963, called *Interaction of Color* "primarily pedagogical." Judd went on with a mixture of moderate, pseudo-Hemingwayesque adulation—"The book makes, to put it simply, one unqualified point, that color is important in art. It does this very well."—and bizarre, incomprehensible disparagement: "The *Interaction of Color* is the best that can be done. It is just that it has all the Biblical possibilities, since it is clear and has limits, of anatomy or of the other subjects whose presence and perfection are supposed to define art. The book should be used but not that way." Albers would never know that Judd would, two decades later, following the older artist's death, rescind these words and make pilgrimages to Albers's studio, feeling that he had not done justice to what *Interaction* was all about and regretting his youthful arrogance. In any event, taking it all in stride, Albers was certainly pleased that an unknown academic at the University of Nevada in Las Vegas had been among those to get the main point, in spades, of *Interaction*: "In an age in which increased human sensibility has become such an obvious need in all areas of human involvement, color sensitivity and awareness can constitute a major weapon against forces of insensitivity and brutalization."

This was the point. The quality of heart, the impact on all of human life, was what Josef Albers sought in his approach. This above all is the reason that we are so pleased that Yale University Press, Josef Albers's partner through thick and thin for five decades, has remained in that role as splendidly as ever. Supportive of the artist's legacy as it was of him during his lifetime when he was in the act of creating, Yale has shown a wonderful and consistent understanding of the brazen, self-generating newness of the artist's approach. Thanks to that fine relationship, Albers's marvelous, unsettling revelations—unsettling to some, exhilarating to others—are again flourishing in this current incarnation of *Interaction of Color*. With its additional plates and refinement of other details, this new, fiftieth-anniversary volume, which effectively updates what is now a "classic," allows Albers's courageous invitation to experimentation, openness, and intellectual and personal expansion to thrive. It invites readers to thrive as well—exactly as Josef Albers would have liked.

Nicholas Fox Weber

Interaction of Color

Introduction

The book "Interaction of Color" is a record of an experimental way of
studying color and of teaching color.

In visual perception a color is almost never seen as it really is
—as it physically is.
This fact makes color the most relative medium in art.

In order to use color effectively it is necessary to recognize
that color deceives continually.
To this end, the beginning is not a study of color systems.

First, it should be learned that one and the same color evokes
innumerable readings.
Instead of mechanically applying or merely implying laws and rules
of color harmony, distinct color effects are produced
—through recognition of the interaction of color—
by making, for instance,
2 very different colors look alike, or nearly alike.

The aim of such study is to develop—through experience
—by trial and error—an eye for color.
This means, specifically, seeing color action
as well as feeling color relatedness.

As a general training it means development of observation and articulation.

This book, therefore, does not follow an academic conception
of "theory and practice."
It reverses this order and places practice before theory,
which, after all, is the conclusion of practice.

Also, the book does not begin with optics and physiology of visual perception,
nor with any presentation of the physics of light and wave length.

Just as the knowledge of acoustics does not make one musical
—neither on the productive nor on the appreciative side—
so no color system by itself can develop one's sensitivity for color.
This is parallel to the recognition that no theory of composition by itself
leads to the production of music, or of art.

Practical exercises demonstrate through color deception (illusion)
the relativity and instability of color.
And experience teaches that in visual perception there is a discrepancy
between physical fact and psychic effect.

What counts here—first and last—is not so-called knowledge
of so-called facts, but vision—seeing.
Seeing here implies Schauen (as in Weltanschauung) and is coupled
with fantasy, with imagination.

This way of searching will lead from a visual realization
of the interaction between color and color
to an awareness of the interdependence of color with form and placement;
with quantity (which measures amount, respectively extension
and / or number, including recurrence);
with quality (intensity of light and / or hue);
and with pronouncement (by separating or connecting boundaries).

The table of contents shows the order
in which exercises usually lead our investigation.

Each exercise is explained and illustrated—
not to give a specific answer,
but to suggest a way of study.

I Color recollection—visual memory

If one says "Red" (the name of a color)
and there are 50 people listening,
it can be expected that there will be 50 reds in their minds.
And one can be sure that all these reds will be very different.

Even when a certain color is specified which all listeners have seen
innumerable times—such as the red of the Coca-Cola signs which is
the same red all over the country—they will still think of
many different reds.

Even if all the listeners have hundreds of reds in front of them
from which to choose the Coca-Cola red, they will again select
quite different colors. And no one can be sure that he has found
the precise red shade.

And even
if that round red Coca-Cola sign with the white name in the middle
is actually shown so that everyone focuses on the same red,
each will receive the same projection on his retina,
but no one can be sure whether each has the same perception.

When we consider further the associations and reactions
which are experienced in connection with the color and the name,
probably everyone will diverge again in many different directions.

What does this show?

First, it is hard, if not impossible, to remember distinct colors.
This underscores the important fact that the visual memory is very poor
in comparison with our auditory memory. Often the latter is able
to repeat a melody heard only once or twice.

Second, the nomenclature of color is most inadequate.
Though there are innumerable colors—shades and tones—
in daily vocabulary, there are only about 30 color names.

II Color reading and contexture

The concept that "the simpler the form of a letter the simpler its reading"
was an obsession of beginning constructivism. It became something
like a dogma, and is still followed by "modernistic" typographers.

This notion has proved to be wrong, because in reading we do not read
letters but words, words as a whole, as a "word picture."
This was discovered in psychology, particularly in Gestalt psychology.
Ophthalmology has disclosed that the more the letters are differentiated
from each other, the easier is the reading.

Without going into comparisons and details, it should be realized that words
consisting of only capital letters present the most difficult reading—
because of their equal height, equal volume, and, with most, their equal width.
When comparing serif letters with sans-serif, the latter provide an uneasy reading.
The fashionable preference for sans-serif in text shows neither historical
nor practical competence.

First, sans-serifs were designed as letters not for texts but for captions,
when pictorial reproductions were introduced with stone lithography.
Second, they produce poor "word pictures."

INTERACTION OF COLOR   Interaction of Color

INTERACTION OF COLOR   Interaction of Color

This illustrates that clear reading depends upon the recognition of context.

In musical compositions,
so long as we hear merely single tones, we do not hear music.
Hearing music depends on the recognition of the in-between of the tones,
of their placing and of their spacing.

In writing, a knowledge of spelling has nothing to do with an understanding
of poetry.

Equally, a factual identification of colors within a given painting
has nothing to do with a sensitive seeing
nor with an understanding of the color action within the painting.

Our study of color differs fundamentally from a study which anatomically
dissects colorants (pigments) and physical qualities (wave length).

Our concern is the interaction of color; that is, seeing
what happens between colors.

We are able to hear a single tone.
But we almost never (that is, without special devices) see a single color
unconnected and unrelated to other colors.
Colors present themselves in continuous flux, constantly related to
changing neighbors and changing conditions.

As a consequence, this proves for the reading of color
what Kandinsky often demanded for the reading of art:
what counts is not the what but the how.

III Why color paper— instead of pigment and paint

When, more than 20 years ago, this systematic study of color was begun,
it occurred almost as a matter of course that the studies would be done
in color papers. At that same time there was some concern among teachers
that students might be reluctant to substitute paper for paint.
Since then, obviously, the attitude of students—and of teachers—
has changed.

In our studies, color paper is preferred to paint
for several practical reasons. Paper provides innumerable colors
in a large range of shades and tints ready for immediate use.
Though a large collection is needed, it is not expensive to assemble
when one does not rely on large prepared paper sets
representing specific color systems, such as the Munsell or Ostwald Systems
(the least desirable are "tuned" sets, claiming to be failure-proof).

Sources easily accessible for many kinds of color paper are waste strips
found at printers and bookbinders; collections of samples of packing papers,
of wrapping and bag papers, of cover and decoration papers. Also, instead
of full sheets of paper, just cutouts from magazines, from advertisements
and illustrations, from posters, wallpapers, paint samples,
and from catalogues with color reproductions of various materials will do.
Often a collective search for papers and a subsequent exchange of them
among class members will provide a rich but inexpensive color paper "palette."

What are the advantages of working with color paper?
First, color paper avoids unnecessary mixing of paints, which is often difficult,
time-consuming, and tiring. This is true not merely for beginners alone.

Second, by not exposing the student to discouraging failures of mixing
and imperfect matching of spoiled paints and papers, we not only save
time and material, but, more important, gain a continued active interest.

Third, color paper permits a repeated use of precisely the same color without the slightest change in tone, light, or surface quality. It permits repetition without disturbing changes caused by varying application of paint (thinner or thicker—even or uneven); without traces of hand or tool resulting in varying density and intensity.

Fourth, working with color paper rarely demands more equipment than paste (heavy rubber cement is best), and a single-edged razor blade instead of scissors. This eliminates tools and equipment for handling paints, and therefore is easier, cheaper, and more orderly.

Fifth, color paper also protects us from undesired and unnecessary addition of so-called texture (such as brush marks and strokes, incalculable changes from wet to dry, or heavy and loose covering, hard and soft boundaries, etc.) which too often only hides poor color conception or application, or, worse, an insensitive color handling.

There is another valuable advantage in working with color papers instead of with paints: in solving our problems again and again we must find just the right color which demonstrates a desired effect. We can choose from a large collection of tones, displayed in front of us, and can thus constantly compare neighboring and contrasting colors. This offers a training which no palette can provide.

IV A color has many faces— the relativity of color

Imagine in front of us 3 pots containing water, from left to right:

<u>WARM</u>   LUKEWARM   <u>COLD</u>

When the hands are dipped first into the outer containers,
one feels—experiences—perceives—2 different temperatures:

<u>WARM</u> (at left)   (at right) <u>COLD</u>

Then dipping both hands
into the middle container,
one perceives again
2 different temperatures,
this time, however,
in reversed order

(at left) <u>COLD</u>—<u>WARM</u> (at right)

though the water is neither of these temperatures, but of another, namely

<u>LUKEWARM</u>

Herewith one experiences
a discrepancy between physical fact and psychic effect called,
in this case, a haptic illusion—haptic as related to the sense of
touch—the haptic sense.

In much the same way as haptic sensations deceive us, so
optical illusions deceive. They lead us to "see" and to "read"
other colors than those with which we are confronted physically.

To begin the study of how color deceives and how to make use of this,
the first exercise is
to make one and the same color look different.

On the blackboard and in our notebooks we write:
Color is the most relative medium in art.

Challenging examples of very surprising color changes are shown.
Then the class is invited to produce similar effects
but is not given reasons or favorable conditions.
It starts, therefore, on a trial-and-error basis.

Thus, continuing comparison—observation—"thinking in situations"—
is promoted, making the class aware that discovery and invention
are the criteria of creativeness.

As a practical study we ask that 2 small rectangles of the same color
and the same size be placed on large grounds of very different color.

Soon, these first trials are collected and separated into groups
of more and less promise.
The class will become aware that change is a result of influence.
The influencing color is distinguished from the influenced color.

It is discovered that certain colors are hard to change, and
that there are others more susceptible to change.

We try to find those colors which are more inclined to exert influence
and to distinguish them from those which will accept influence.

A second class exhibition of more advanced results should clarify
that there are 2 kinds of changing influences working in 2 directions,
light on the one side and hue on the other. And both occur simultaneously—
though in varying strength.

Since 2 pieces of the same paper, therefore of the same color,
are to appear different—and, if possible, incredibly different—
we must compare them under equal conditions.
The only colors which are factually different are the large grounds,
though they are alike in size and shape.

Because of the laboratory character of these studies
there is no opportunity to decorate, to illustrate, to represent anything,
or to express something—or one's self.

Here, successful studies present a demonstration. Since they cannot be
misread or misunderstood, they prove understanding both
of the principle involved and of the materials to be manipulated.
(See plates IV-1 and IV-3.)

It should be clear that, with these exercises and all others to follow, whether or not we arrive at a pleasant or harmonious color combination is unimportant.

Precision and clean execution are required for all finished studies. To avoid destroying the desired effect, small pieces of paper on small grounds should not be used.
Arrangements such as the one shown below disguise the desired effect and lead to confusion:

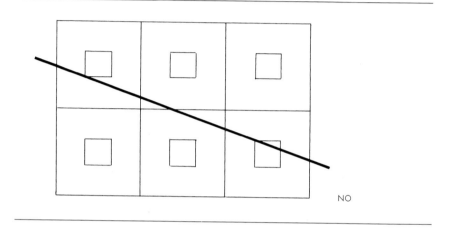

NO

Such studies shown separately in pairs may demonstrate clearly
the desired effects. But interlocked in the tile pattern opposite,
their illusional effects annul each other because of:

> a) The simultaneous influence from too many directions—
>   from left and right, and above and below;
> b) The unfavorable distribution of area between the influencing
>   and the influenced color.

Consequently, such presentation lacks both sight and insight.

YES

V Lighter and / or darker— light intensity, lightness

If one is not able to distinguish the difference between a higher tone
and a lower tone, one probably should not make music.

If a parallel conclusion were to be applied to color, almost everyone
would prove incompetent for its proper use. Very few are able to distinguish
higher and lower light intensity (usually called higher and lower value)
between different hues. This is true despite our daily reading of numerous
black-and-white pictures.

Since the discovery of photography and particularly since the development
of photomechanical reproduction processes, we are exposed—more and more
every day—to pictures from all over the world, the world seen and unseen,
visible and invisible.

These pictures, which are predominantly "black and white,"
are printed in only 1 black on a white ground. Visually, however,
these pictures consist of grey shades of the finest gradations
between the poles of black and white. These shades penetrate each other
in varying degrees.

With the tremendous increase in pictorial information
—through newspapers, magazines, books—we receive a training
in the reading of lighter and darker tones of grey as has never before
existed. With the growing interest in color photography and color reproduction,
a parallel training in the reading of lighter and darker color is on the way.

However, it is still true that only a minority can distinguish
the lighter from the darker within close intervals
when obscured by contrasting hues or by different color intensities.

In order to correct a prejudice common among painters and designers—
that they belong to that minority—
we have the students test themselves. We confront them
with several pairs of color, from which they are to select and to record
which color in a pair is the darker.

The darker one, it is explained, is visually the heavier one, or the one containing more black, or less white. It should be mentioned that the students are encouraged to abstain from making a judgment in any case of doubt. It may also demonstrate that not voting can have a positive meaning.

Though there have always been advanced painting students in the basic color class, the result of this test has remained constant for a number of years: 60% of the answers are wrong and only 40% are right, not counting the undecided cases.

By this experience we are led to the next task: To find colors about which we cannot say immediately which is the lighter or darker. These colors are collected and pasted in pairs, and observed again and again until their light-dark relationship is clearly recognized.

In cases where a decision seems impossible, an after-image effect may be helpful. 2 color sheets are put on top of each other in this way:

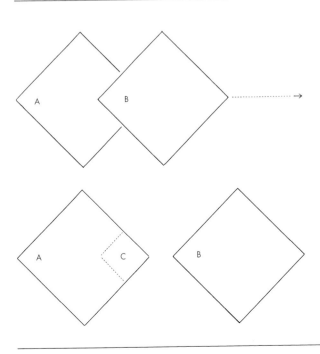

Focus longer than the eye wants to on the covering corner (B) of the
upper paper and then quickly remove this upper sheet. If area (C)
now appears lighter than area (A), then the upper paper is the darker—
and vice versa. After this, repeat the experiment with the papers in
reverse order. Frequently only 1 of the 2 reversed comparisons
reveals the true relationship.

The usual results (60% wrong) are disillusioning as well as revealing.
Voting for the wrong color often needs cover or compensation; also,
the disappointment of wrong answers encourages doubts.
The doubts often are directed, not against one's own judgment, but against
the competence of the teacher: are his answers the right ones?

As the test is to prove whether one has a trained eye or not,
the pairs of color presented for discrimination are not easy to decipher.
Within the pairs there is no equal light intensity
because the conclusive question to be expected from a class is:
are there equal light values within these couples?
The answer is No.

Another unavoidable question is: will a photograph of these colors
reveal their true relationship and thus give the final proof?
The answer again is No.

This answer will remain true for black-and-white
as well as color photographs, because the sensitivity
and consequently the registration of the retina of an eye is different
from the sensitivity and registration of a photographic film.

Normally, black-and-white photography registers all lights lighter
and all darks darker than the more adjustable eye perceives them.
The eye also distinguishes better the so-called middle greys,
which in photography often are flattened if not lost.

As an example we showed our class 2 different reproductions of the
same Ensor painting, "Masks Confronting Death," of 1888. The first
appeared in the catalogue of an Ensor exhibition, the other in a
newspaper report on the same exhibition.

The first, the larger and more official reproduction, in very fine screen
on coated paper, presumably would be considered more representative than
the second, smaller reproduction in a coarser screen and on the
cheapest paper.

But the latter was not only much more correct in its whole tonality;
it also showed clearly 1 more mask, face, or head which the more
expensive, so-called high-key reproduction blotted out entirely—a small
but complete frontal face, lighter than all the others and separated
from them, near the left picture edge.

This shows what a higher key in light can lose in photography.

The greatest advantage the eye has over photography
is its scotopic seeing in addition to its photopic seeing.
The former means, briefly, the retinal adjustment to lower light conditions.

Color photography deviates still more from eye vision
than black-and-white photography. Blue and red are overemphasized
to such an extent that their brightness is exaggerated.
Though this may flatter public taste, the result is a loss
in finer nuances and in delicate relationships.
Whites rarely appear white but usually look greenish.
This makes color slides of Mondrian paintings unbearable.

Gradation studies—new presentations

With the experience that often we are unsure and thus unable
to distinguish between lighter and darker in color, it appears appropriate, even
necessary, to develop a more discriminating sensitivity. To this end,
we study gradation by producing so-called grey steps, grey scales,
grey ladders. These demonstrate a gradual stepping up or down between
white and black, between lighter and darker.

For such exercises, we first collect as many greys in paper as possible,
and preferably independent of commercial grey sets, which usually offer
a too limited choice, or, worse, unequal steps. Rich sources for
many paper greys are black-and-white reproductions from popular magazines.

Selecting from them smaller and larger areas of as many greys as possible, we will be taught first that photography registers and measures light and dark differently from our eyes. That it turns darks darker and lights lighter means, besides a generalization toward the polar contrasts, a loss of the visually more interesting middle greys. Thus, such reproductions confront us with a dominance of very heavy and very light greys, and a consequent scarcity of middle greys.

These cutouts are to be arranged in gradations as described. The softer the steps appear, and the more equal the steps are, the more valuable and convincing the study. As any lines or empty spaces between the steps interfere with a direct comparison, such separating in-betweens prove nonsensical. We also reject the still-recommended but misleading stepping-up of the thin layers of water colors or India ink, as explained in Chapter xx. In order to avoid such mistakes, and also any mechanical repetition of the too-familiar illustrations of color books, we aim at a more creative, more challenging, more instructive presentation. Thus we subdivide and mount our grey scales to show new interactions, particularly between graduating and non-graduating greys, and vice versa. (See plate v-1.)

Color intensity—brightness

After the study of "Lighter or Darker" and with some training in gradation studies, one can expect to come to an agreement on different light intensities.

However, when it comes to color intensity (brightness), occasionally one may find agreement among a few people but hardly within a large group such as a class.

As "gentlemen prefer blondes," so everyone has preference for certain colors
and prejudices against others. This applies to color combinations as well.
It seems good that we are of different tastes.
As it is with people in our daily life, so it is with color.
We change, correct, or reverse our opinions about colors, and this change
of opinion may shift forth and back.

Therefore, we try to recognize our preferences and our aversions—
what colors dominate in our work; what colors, on the other hand,
are rejected, disliked, or of no appeal. Usually a special effort
in using disliked colors ends with our falling in love with them.

The exercise in color intensity consists of sorting
all possible shades and tints within a hue. From these is chosen
the most typical hue (the bluest blue, the greenest green, etc.)
and it is placed within the group accordingly. (See plate v-3.)

VI 1 color appears as 2 —
looking like the reversed grounds

Having presented, in the previous problem, a very detailed explanation
of a step-by-step method of teaching and learning, the following problem
permits a briefer description.

With the first exercise in color interaction we make
>   1 color look like 2, or, what means the same,
>   3 colors look like 4. The next step is to make
>   3 colors look like 2, or, describing it as in the previous task,
>   1 color is to show 2 faces which refer to the 2 colors
>   of the reversed grounds,
>   or, the changed color is to echo the 2 changing ones.

After showing a few examples, the task of producing similar effects
is introduced with the question:
>   Which color will play simultaneously the roles
>   of the 2 colors of the 2 reciprocal grounds?

The first class exhibition of preliminary solutions shows that most of the
trial colors selected appear closer to one ground than to the other.

However, when one tries to find a color that is equally close
or equally distant from both grounds, one will discover that
even a large collection of color paper (even that of the entire class)
may not provide the fitting tone.

Then, instead of pushing the in-between color to one or the other side,
we must consider changing 1 or both of the grounds, either moving
closer to or more distant from the in-between color. (See diagram.)

After repeated trials it must be concluded that the only fitting color
is the one which is topologically in the middle of the colors
of the 2 grounds.

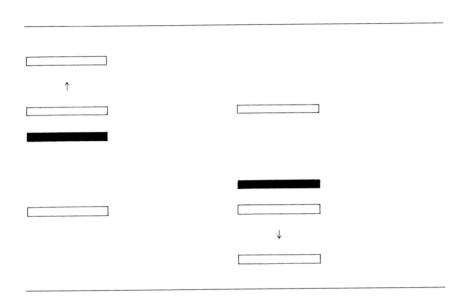

The task is to find this middle color.

This is relatively easy when the 2 grounds are of the same hue,
as with a lighter and a darker green ground,
or with a lighter and a darker violet ground.

It is a more challenging task to find the middle color
between 2 different hues
but it is particularly interesting when the 2 grounds
are of opposing (complementary) colors. (See plates VI-3 and VI-4.)

VII 2 different colors look alike —
subtraction of color

The fact that one and the same color can perform many different roles
is well known and is consciously applied.

Less well known is the possibility in the previous exercise
of giving a color the look of reversed grounds.

Still more exciting is the next task, the reverse of the first:
to make 2 different colors look alike.

In the first exercise it was learned that the more different
the grounds, the stronger is their changing influence.

It has been seen that color differences are caused by 2 factors:
by hue and by light, and in most cases by both at the same time.

Recognizing this, one is able to "push" light and / or hue,
by the use of contrasts, away from their first appearance
toward the opposite qualities.
Since this amounts virtually to adding opposite qualities,
it follows that one might achieve parallel effects
by subtracting those qualities not desired.

This new experience can be achieved first by observing
3 small samples of 3 reds on a white ground.
They will appear first of all—red.

Then when the 3 reds are placed on a ground of another red
their differences, which are differences of hue as well as of light,
will become more obvious.

Third, when placed on a red ground equal to 1 of the 3 samples,
only 2 of the reds will "show," and the lost one is absorbed—subtracted.
Repeated similar experiments with adjacent colors will show
that any ground subtracts its own hue from colors which it carries
and therefore influences.

Additional experiments with light colors on light grounds
and dark colors on dark grounds prove that the light of a ground
subtracts in the same way that its hue does.

From this, it follows that any diversion among colors
in hue as well as in light-dark relationship
can be reduced if not obliterated visually on grounds
of equal qualities.

Such studies provide a broad training in analytical comparison
and usually evoke surprising results, leading the student
to an intense study of color. (See plates VII-4, VII-5, and VII-7.)

VIII Why color deception?—
after-image, simultaneous contrast

For a better understanding of why colors read differently
from what they really (physically) are, we show now
the cause of most color illusions.

In order to prepare for the second part of this demonstration, cut out in
red and white color paper 2 equal circles (of ca. 3-inch diameter)
and mark their centers with a small black dot.
(See plate VIII-1.)

Then paste them—horizontally related—the red circle to
the left and the white one to the right, on the blackboard or
a piece of black paper or black cardboard, ca. 10 inches high and
20 inches long, with about equal amounts of black before, between,
and after the 2 circles.

Now, by staring steadily at the marked center of the red
circle (up to half a minute) one soon discovers how difficult
it is to keep the eye fixed on a point. After a while,
moon-sickle shapes appear, moving along the circle's
periphery. In spite of this, one must continue to focus on
the red center point in order to assure the desired experience.
Then quickly shift the focus to the center of the white circle.

From the class one usually hears noises which indicate
surprise or astonishment. This happens because all normal eyes
suddenly see green or blue-green instead of white. This green
is the complementary color of red or red-orange.
The phenomenon of seeing green (in this case) instead of white
is called after-image, or simultaneous contrast.

A plausible explanation:

One theory maintains that the nerve ends on the human retina (rods and cones)
are tuned to receive any of the 3 primary colors (red, yellow,
or blue), which constitute all colors.

Staring at red will fatigue the red-sensitive parts, so that with
a sudden shift to white (which again consists of red, yellow, and blue),
only the mixture of yellow and blue occurs. And this is green,
the complement of red.

The fact that the after-image or simultaneous contrast
is a psycho-physiological phenomenon should prove
that no normal eye, not even the most trained one, is foolproof
against color deception.
He who claims to see colors independent of their illusionary changes
fools only himself, and no one else.

IX Color mixture in paper— illusion of transparence

It is obvious that in working with color paper there is no way
of mixing the colors mechanically, as paint and pigment permit,
and as they invite one to do on a palette or in a container.

Though this may first appear as a handicap, it is actually a challenge
to study color mixture in our imagination, that is, so to say,
with closed eyes.

Starting with the simple and well-known fact that blue and yellow
when mixed produce green, a blue and yellow are selected
and held next to each other. One tries to imagine what kind of green
would result from a mixture of these 2 colors.
Then a paper is selected appropriate to this imagined mixture.

In order to find out whether the "thought-out" mixture is acceptable—
believable—convincing—the 3 colors (2 "color parents" and
1 "color descendant") are placed in 3 equal rectangles as follows:

Blue horizontally (1), green vertically (2)
so that its upper part overlaps the blue. The yellow is put on top
of the green (3) so that its top edge coincides with the bottom edge of the blue.

In such placement, the green will be the "in-between" of the other colors
and thus their mixture.

After the class has found several believable mixtures, these are collected
for an exhibition (most practically, on the floor) and the most convincing ones
are selected. Some are usually more successful than others. The class states
their merits and shortcomings and suggests possible corrections and improvements.

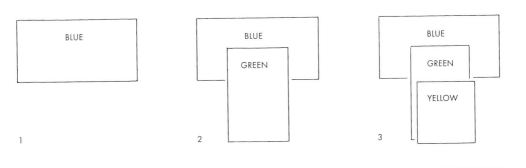

1   2   3

By means of the exhibition, the students will be reminded that there are many blues and many yellows, and will conclude that there are innumerable mixtures descending from them. It is obvious that any 2 colors can produce many mixtures.

In addition to the illusion of mixture, another deception will be recognized— that, in an illusionary mixture in paper, 1 color seems to show through the other. The "mixture" paper, therefore, loses its opacity and appears transparent or translucent.

In order to make the eye read this double illusion of mixture and of transparence, the colors must be placed in overlapping shapes.

In the drawing on page 26 the hatched parts belong to each of the overlapping shapes and are therefore the logical place for the mixture.

After simple mixtures, such as blue and yellow producing green—red and blue producing violet—black and white producing grey—less common pairs, such as pink and ochre, present a further challenge.

For a more intensive experience, keep the area of the mixture larger than those of the 2 mixing ones. (See plate IX-1.)

If we name 2 mixture parents A and B, and their mixture C,
then our first task is to find C's, which are mixtures of A and B,
another task will be "   "   B's, conditioned by   A "   C,
or, a third task,   "   "   A's   "   "   B "   C.

This invites one to draw conclusions backward, that is, to guess—
from a mixture and 1 mixture parent—the other mixture parent.

X Factual mixtures—
additive and subtractive

Though the color class (as a rule) abstains from the use of colorants
(meaning pigments and paints) for reasons explained before,
the color studies in paper are related to the actual use of paint
as often as possible.

Therefore, after the introductory studies of mixture as illusion,
factual mixing is analyzed. There are 2 kinds of physical mixture:
  a)   Direct mixture of projected light,
  b)   Indirect mixture of reflected light.

a)   Color light, or direct color, probably is most familiar
        through its practical application in theater and advertising.
        The scientific analysis of the physical qualities (wave length, etc.)
        is not the problem of the colorist; it is the concern of the physicist.
        When he mixes his colors, he projects them on a screen,
        1 on top of or overlapping the other.
        In any such mixture where there is overlapping,
        it will be obvious that every one of these mixtures
        is lighter than any of the mixture parents.
        By means of a prismatic lens, the physicist easily demonstrates
        that the color spectrum of the rainbow is a dispersion of the white sunlight.
        With this he proves also that the sum of all colors in light is white.
        This demonstrates an additive mixture.

b)   When pigment or paint is mixed on a palette or in a container
        it is seen by the eye as reflected light.
        This mixing will never result in white as the sum of colors.
        On the contrary, the more color that is mixed, the more the mixture approaches
        a dark grey leaning toward black. This we call subtractive mixture.
        Also, the psychologist, who mixes colors of reflecting colorants
        optically on the rotating wheel, is not able to arrive at mixtures
        lighter than the lighter color parent of the mixture.

As optical mixture usually means less loss of light
than mechanical mixture, the psychologist's sum of all his colors
normally approaches a middle grey instead of the dark grey of the painter.

The conclusion is: mixtures gain light only in direct color, as in (a),
whereas mixtures of reflected colors lose light, as in (b).

Though direct color or color light normally is not the medium of the colorist,
examples of this effect should be indicated. Additive and subtractive mixtures
should be made in appropriate studies in transparence illusions. These will
provide a preparatory training for studies to follow.

For the sake of simplicity and to avoid difficult complications, these mixtures
should be done in 1 thin color mixing preferably with white (or black),
and then reversing the first study. (See plate x-1.)

Sample arrangements:

AND REVERSED   AND REVERSED

XI Transparence and space-illusion
Color boundaries and plastic action

A study of color mixture in paper leads to 3 important discoveries.

First, under normal conditions, a subtractive mixture is not as light
as the lighter of the color parents nor as dark as the darker one.
Furthermore, the mixture is reciprocally neither higher nor lower
in color intensity than the color parents.

Second, a mixture depends upon the proportion in which colors are mixed.
Varying amounts of blue and yellow, for instance, define the character
of a green. This indicates a possible predominance of 1 color parent.

Third, when 1 color is read as appearing above or below another
in the transparence studies, a third deception is recognized—space-illusion.

This leads to the next task:
To produce different illusionary mixtures which derive from 1 pair
of parent colors. If the parents are again a blue and a yellow,
some greens will be found with yellow dominance
and others with blue dominance. With more mixing experience
it will become apparent that the nearness of a mixture to one side
(let us say yellow) necessitates distance from the opposite side
(in this case blue).

After having found several mixtures of different pairs of parent colors,
we then try to find the most significant and the most difficult mixture
—the middle mixture. Topographically, this middle mixture demands
precise placement, and therefore additional means of measure are necessary.

Since the middle mixture presupposes equidistance from the color parents,
it therefore depends equally upon the absence of any predominance
of the color parents.

Here, the following diagrams may be helpful:

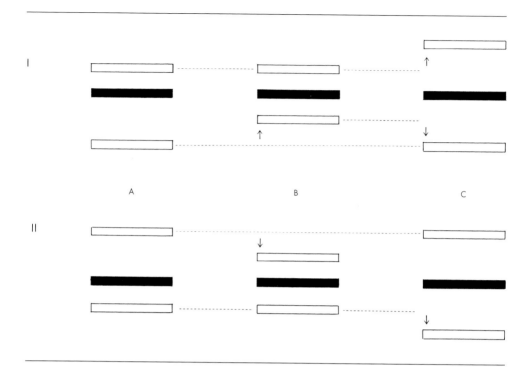

A   B   C

Of the 3 bars in each diagram, the black bar represents
an in-between color, the mixture in question; that is, the one
to be "equidistant" from the accompanying white bars.
The latter represent possible color parents for a color mixture.
The upper bar represents a lighter (higher) color,
and the lower bar represents a deeper (heavier) color.

In Iᴀ the mixture line is nearer to the upper line, and is therefore too light;
in IIᴀ the opposite happens. The middle color-to-be is nearer to the
lower bar and consequently is too dark. For the necessary corrections
in Iᴀ, we must look for a lower (darker) middle, and in IIᴀ for a higher
(lighter) middle.

Unfortunately, those higher and lower tones are often not available.
In such cases, we should try to adjust the outer (upper or lower) colors
—instead of the middle color—in order to exercise another way
of correct placement.

Thus, in I**b** the lower bar is lifted from the dotted line,
e.g. a lighter color is chosen; in II**b** the upper bar is lowered.
In **c** similar changes take place but in an
opposite direction from **b**. Comparing groups **b** and **c** will
demonstrate that correct arrangements may become closer to or more distant
from the middle color.

Such efforts forth and back in our search for a middle color—
to be specific, for a middle placement—provide through
continued comparison a thorough visual training:
"thinking in situations."

Besides an explanation of the above diagrams on the blackboard,
a physical demonstration in space may clarify this further.
When discussing the first trial studies, exhibited on the floor
with the students standing around them, 2 hands held horizontally
1 above the other may act as the 2 outer colors.
And a third hand held between them may demonstrate various possibilities
of color selection and placement, either by moving the hand indicating
the middle color up or down, or by moving the outer hands up
and / or down, singly or together.

With a more developed sensitivity for mixtures, it will be discovered
that distance, nearness, and equidistance between colors
can be recognized through the boundaries between the mixture and the mixture parents.

By exercising comparison and distinction of color boundaries, a new and
important measure is gained for the reading of the plastic action of color,
that is, for the spatial organization of color.
Since softer boundaries disclose nearness implying connection,
harder boundaries indicate distance, separation.

In both interpretations colors are placed above or below each other,
or in front of or behind each other. They are read as here and there,
as over, and beyond there, and therefore in space.

All this seems to change with colors producing middle mixtures. Sometimes
they appear as if meeting within a 2-dimensional plane; at other times
they can be read—interchangeably—as higher or lower than the mixture.

Thus, with a middle mixture all boundaries are equally soft or hard.
As a consequence, a middle mixture appears frontal, as a color by itself.
This is comparable to the reading of any symmetrical order
and the middle mixture will behave unspatially,
unless its own shape, or surrounding shapes, decides differently.
(See plates XI-1 and XI-3.)

Such a study, or a similar recognition, in my opinion, led Cézanne
to his unique and new articulation in painting. He was the first
to develop color areas which produce both distinct and indistinct endings
—areas connected and unconnected—areas with and without boundaries—
as means of plastic organization.

And, in order to prevent evenly painted areas from looking flat and frontal,
he used emphasized borders sparingly, mainly where he needed
a spatial separation from adjacent color areas.

XII   Optical mixture—after-image revised

XIII   The Bezold Effect

In contrast to after-image, so far the main concern of our studies, here
is another very different color illusion called "optical mixture."
Instead of 2 (or more) colors changing each other, "pulling" or "pushing"
each other into different appearances (toward both greater difference and greater
similarity), here 2 colors (or more), perceived simultaneously, are seen
combined and thus merged into 1 new color. In this process, the 2
original colors are first annulled and made invisible, and then replaced by
a substitute called optical mixture.

From the Impressionist painters we have learned that they never presented, let us say,
green by itself. Instead of using green paint mixed mechanically from yellow
and blue, they applied yellow and blue unmixed in small dots, so that they
became mixed only in our perception—as an impression. That the dots
mentioned were small indicates that this effect depends on size and on distance.

The discovery of the mixing of colors in our perception led in the last
century not only to the new painting technique of the Impressionists, and
particularly of the Pointillists, but also to the invention of new photomechanical
reproduction techniques, the 3- and 4-color process for paintings, and the
halftone process for black-and-white pictures. In the first case, 3 or 4
color plates subdivided into tiny printing dots mix to innumerable color
shades and tints. In the second case, a plate for black also subdivided by
a screen in tiny dots mixes with the white paper in just as innumerable
tones of white—grey—black.

There is a special kind of optical mixture, the Bezold Effect, named after its
discoverer, Wilhelm von Bezold (1837–1907). He recognized
this effect when searching for a method through which he could change the
color combinations of his rug designs entirely by adding or changing 1 color only.
Apparently, there is so far no clear recognition of the optical-
perceptual conditions involved. (See plates XIII-1, XIII-2, and XIII-3.)

XIV Color intervals and transformation

The tune of "Good morning to you" consists of 4 tones. It can be sung
in a high soprano, a low basso, and in all in-between voices, as well as
on many levels and in many keys. It can be played on innumerable instruments.

In all possible ways of performance, this melody will keep its character
and it will be recognized instantly.

Why? The intervals of the 4 tones, that is, their acoustical
constellation (again comparable with a topographical relationship),
remains the same.

Although it is not common practice, one can also speak of intervals
between colors.
Colors and hues are defined, as are tones in music, by wave length.

Any color (shade or tint) always has 2 decisive characteristics:
color intensity (brightness) and light intensity (lightness).
Therefore, color intervals also have this double-sidedness, this duality.

As has been stated before, after some training one might easily agree
on light relationship, that is, which of 2 colors is lighter
and which is darker. However, there is rarely agreement on color intensity,
that is, which among a number of reds is the reddest red.
For this reason the interval transformation exercise is concerned mainly
with light intensity.

To prepare a basic exercise in color transformation, combine
4 equal squares of different colors to make 1 larger square.
Within this grouping of 4 squares, the lighter will differentiate
from the heavier, darker color. Therefore, the squares will connect
with each other or separate according to contrast and affinity,
as vertical, horizontal, or diagonal pairs, or as a trio forming
an angle, embracing or opposing a fourth square. (See diagrams.)

34

The task is to transfer these specific relationships to a higher or lower key
within 2 or more groups of equally large rectangles. Of course,
if the first group contains the darkest color available, one cannot go lower.
Similarly, the lightest white would not permit any transference to
a higher key.

It is rarely possible to retain the first 4 rectangles selected.
Frequently it will be impossible to find 4 colors equally raised
or lowered when compared with the original set. If so, the original set
should be changed in order to transfer more successfully.

In a successful study, both groups should show equal relationships
in equal placement, as a constellation. Then, as with the study of
varying mixtures, the boundaries between the 4 rectangles
will also appear similar in both groups.

Again, the aim of this exercise is not to present a pleasant, perhaps harmonious look,
but to present a study aiming at one distinct relationship—
parallel intervals.

How do we prove such similarity, such parallelism?
As has been learned from gradation studies done at the beginning, it is
poor "psychological engineering" to present the gradation steps
unconnected, that is, separated by black lines. Similarly, in the transformation
exercise it is hard to compare the boundaries within the
original group of 4 rectangles with the raised or lowered boundaries in
the second, separated group.

The only way in which the 2 groups can be compared easily and accurately is to superimpose 1 group on the other.

For this purpose we cut from the center of the first group a small rectangle and exchange it with an equally shaped and placed small rectangle of the second group. (See diagrams below.)

Immediately, the superimposed rectangles will show whether the stepping up or down within 1 group corresponds with the stepping in the other. A further comparison should be made between each small rectangle and the larger group beneath it. The sample studies will also show that the boundaries provide an important means of comparison.

Usually, as shown, a lower color tetrachord is transferred to a higher key, or opposite; one may also break with habit and try to make a low color constellation still lower, or a high one still higher. (See plates XIV-1, XIV-2, and XIV-3.)

By keeping the stepping—up or down—small, a special effect of transparence is achieved called film color, to be described in Chapter XVII.

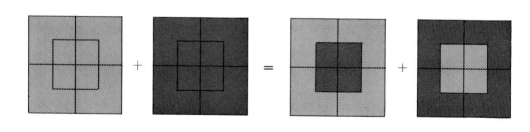

XV The middle mixture again— intersecting colors

Our studies of illusionary transparence have shown how difficult it is
to find a middle mixture.

A true middle mixture is distinguished by being equidistant
—in light and in hue—
from either mixture parent.

Unfortunately, for an untrained eye, it is hard to recognize
such equidistance.
We have seen that the color boundaries between the mixing color
and the mixed one have proved to be helpful measures.

The purpose of the new problem, intersecting colors,
is to show and to produce a certain constellation
by which even an untrained eye will recognize
within a mixture not only the constituents
but also their respective amounts within that mixture.

For an initial experience in this direction
find 3 equally large sheets of 1 red in 3 shades,
a light red, the same red darker, and the almost always elusive
middle mixture of these reds. Or, if not available in red,
take any other color providing a lighter, a middle, and
a darker shade or tint. (See diagrams, next page.)

Place them adjacent to one another,
with the lighter red to the left and overlapped by the edge of the middle red;
then place the dark red on top of the middle red, allowing only a narrow strip
of the middle red (about ¼ inch wide) to remain visible.

Then, very slowly, pull the dark sheet to the right,
gradually making the narrow strip of the middle red wider.

By staring at the middle red, observe that the wider it grows, the more it appears
not as 1 but as 2 colors, becoming lighter and lighter
at the right edge, and, at the same time, darker and darker
at the left edge.

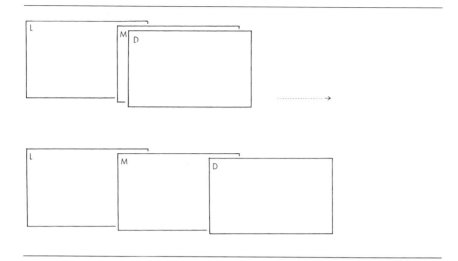

By doing this repeatedly, it becomes obvious that the middle color
plays the role of both mixture parents, presenting them
in reversed placement.

Repeating this experience with other colors will show that
in a true middle mixture the mixture parents will appear
in equal amounts.

In most cases, however, the larger amount of 1 of the 2 colors
reveals its predominance.

Such exercises are exciting as well as revealing, particularly
when extended to different and opposing colors.

These exercises remind us that the basic after-image presentation,
the simultaneous contrast, is the cause of all color deception.

Whereas the first measuring of middle mixtures led us
to space illusion through connecting and separating boundaries,
this direct reading of the mixture constituents leads us
to a new deception: an illusion of volume.

It is an effect we have seen in the channelings of the Doric column
and is called a fluting effect. (See plate xv-2.)

XVI Color juxtaposition— harmony—quantity

Harmony

Color systems usually lead to the conclusion
that certain constellations within a system provide color harmony.
They indicate that this is mainly the aim and the end
of color combination, of color juxtaposition.

As harmony and harmonizing is also a concern of music, so
a parallelism of effect between tone combinations and color combinations
seems unavoidable and appropriate. Although
a comparison of composed colors with composed tones is very challenging,
it should be mentioned that, while it can be helpful,
it is often misleading.

This is because different basic conditions of these media result in
different behavior.

Tones appear placed and directed predominantly in time from <u>before</u>
to <u>now</u> to <u>later</u>.

Their juxtaposition in a musical composition is perceived
within a prescribed sequence only. Vertically, so to say,
1 tone, or several simultaneously,
sound for a varying but restricted length of time.
Horizontally, the tones follow each other,
perhaps not in a straight line, but of necessity in a prescribed order
and only in 1 direction—forward.
Tones heard earlier fade, and those farther back disappear, vanish.
We do not hear them backward.

Colors appear connected predominantly in space. Therefore,
as constellations they can be seen in any direction and
at any speed. And as they remain, we can return to them repeatedly
and in many ways.

This remaining and not remaining, or vanishing and not vanishing,
shows only 1 essential difference between the fields of tone
and color.

The accuracy of perception in one field is matched
by the durability of retention in the other, demonstrating
a curious reversal in visual and auditory memory.

Tone juxtapositions can be defined by their acoustical relationship
and thus measured precisely by wave length.

Consequently, a graphic registration of tones in musical composition
has been developed.

Color, also, can be measured, at least to some extent,
and particularly so when it is presented as direct color—
as the physicist registers it, by optical wave length.

Reflected color, however, coming from paint and pigment
—our main medium—is much more difficult to define.

When analyzed with an electrical spectrograph
reflected color shows that it contains all visible wave lengths.
Therefore, any reflected color—not just white —
consists of all other colors.

This many-sided relationship between colors is clearly visible
in the plates of a 4-color reproduction, when singly shown,
because each of the 4 plates, although presenting only 1 color,
shows a complete picture.

Color, when practically applied, not only appears in uncountable
shades and tints, but is additionally characterized
by shape and size, by recurrence and placement, and so on, of which
particularly shape and size are not directly applicable
to tones.

All this may signify why any color composition naturally defies
such diagrammatic registration as notation in music
and choreography in dance.

With regard to constellation, tone intervals, such as third, fifth, and octave,
differentiate exact vertical distance. We say "vertical" probably because
tones are described as low and high.
Slide deflections (aberrations), such as in flat and sharp,
remain equally precise.
Color terms which could be considered parallel to tone intervals
are complementaries, split complementaries, triads, tetrads, and octads.
Though these characterize distance and constellation within color systems,
their deflections, such as incomplete triads and incomplete tetrads,
indicate that their measure is only arbitrary.

Significantly, complementaries, though they are the basic color contrast
or interval, are topographically quite vague.

In principle, a complementary is a color accompanied by its after-image.

However, the complement of a specific color, when placed
in different systems, will look different.

Similarly, a triad or tetrad of one system will hardly fit
into another system.

Usually, illustrations of harmonic color constellations which derive
from authoritative systems look pleasant, beautiful, and thus convincing.
But it should not be overlooked that they are usually presented in a
most theoretical and least practicable manner, because normally
all harmony members appear in the same quantity and the same shape,
as well as in the same number (just once) and sometimes even in similar
light intensity.
Such outer equalization may unify them, but at the expense
of the more important inner relatedness—namely, as color only.

When applied in practice, these harmony sets appear changed.
In addition to quantity, form, and recurrence,
wider aspects exert still more changing influences.
These are:

>Changed and changing light—and, even worse,
several simultaneous lights;
reflection of lights and of colors;
direction and sequence of reading;
presentation in varying materials;
constant or altering juxtaposition of related
and unrelated objects.

With these and other visual displacements, it should not be a surprise
that the sympathetic effect of the original "ideal" color combination
often appears changed, lost, and reversed.

Observe the interior and exterior, the furniture and textile decoration
following such color schemes, as well as commercialized color "suggestions"
for innumerable do-it-yourselves.

Our conclusion: we may forget for a while those rules of thumb
of complementaries, whether complete or "split," and of triads and
tetrads as well.
They are worn out.

Second, no mechanical color system is flexible enough
to precalculate the manifold changing factors, as named before,
in a single prescribed recipe.

Good painting, good coloring, is comparable to good cooking.
Even a good cooking recipe demands tasting and repeated tasting
while it is being followed.
And the best tasting still depends on a cook with taste.

By giving up preference for harmony,
we accept dissonance to be as desirable as consonance.

In searching for new color organization—color design—
we have come to think that quantity, intensity, or weight, as principles of study,
can lead similarly to illusions, to new relationships, to different measurements,
to other systems, as do transparence, space, and intersection.

Besides a balance through color harmony, which is comparable
to symmetry, there is equilibrium possible between
color tensions, related to a more dynamic asymmetry.

Again: knowledge and its application is not our aim;
instead, it is flexible imagination, discovery, invention—taste.

With this study of color effects, that is, of color deception,
a special interest in quantity—amount as well as recurrence—
has developed.

Quantity

Although quantity and quality often are considered disparate, in art and
music they appear closely related. We may even hear, "Quantity
is a quality," because here quantity not only designates amounts,
as of weight or number, but also is a means of underlining,
of pronouncement, and a means of equilibrium, of balance.

One who particularly recognized the latter was Schopenhauer.
When he tried to improve Goethe's 6-part color circle—to Goethe's dismay—
he changed the previous presentation of 6 equal areas to decidedly
different quantities.

Thus yellow, the lightest color, appears in the smaller amount,
and its opposite, violet, as the darkest, in the largest amount.
He first allotted 3 equal thirds of a color ring to the 3 pairs
of opposites—yellow & violet—blue & orange—red & green.
Second, he subdivided those thirds, for the same order of pairs,
in ¼ + ¾ — ⅓ + ⅔ — ½ + ½. These figures
in fractions of 12ths (relatively 36ths) are proportionate to
3 : 9 — 4 : 8 — 6 : 6 equal parts.
When seen in a color circle, from yellow around to green, they present
the following quantities: 3 : 4 : 6 : 9 : 8 : 6.

The 2 basic quantity questions, how much and how often,
distinguish 2 kinds of quantity:
1 of size—extension in area—and
1 of recurrence—extension in number.
Both measurements concern predominance and emphasis.
They establish weight in space—and weight in time.

Such considerations are both the source and result of our quantity studies
in which 4 colors usually appear in 4 different juxtapositions,
so different that all 4 studies appear as unrelated as possible.

And thus they present changes in climate or temperature,
in tempo or rhythm—that is, changes of atmosphere or mood,
so that the factual contents (the same 4 colors) are hidden or, better,
hardly recognizable.

To use a theatrical parallel:
A set of 4 colors is to be considered—singly as "actors,"
together as "cast." They are to be presented in 4 different
arrangements—as "performances."

Although they remain unchanged in hue and light, in "character,"
and appear in an unchanging outer frame, the "stage,"
they are to produce 4 different "scenes" or "plays,"
each to be so different that one and the same set of colors will be seen as
4 different sets, presented by 4 different casts.

And all this can be achieved mainly through changes in quantity
which result in shifts of dominance, of recurrence, and consequently
of placement.

The essential question: which group of colors is ready to lose
its identity as a cast?

A parallel question: which distribution of appearance
(quantities of space, time, and weight) protects, disguises
recognition of the same color cast?

Such quantity studies have taught us to believe that, independent
of harmony rules, any color "goes" or "works" with any other color,
presupposing that their quantities are appropriate.
We feel fortunate that so far there are no comprehensive rules
for such aims. (See plates XVI-2 and XVI-3.)

Here we may point to a discovery made by a few contemporary painters,
that the increase in amount of a color—not merely in size of canvas—
visually reduces distance. As a consequence, it often produces nearness—
meaning intimacy—and respect.

XVII Film color and volume color—
2 natural effects

Usually, we think of an apple as being red.
This is not the same red as that of a cherry or tomato.
A lemon is yellow and an orange is like its name.
Bricks vary from beige to yellow to orange,
and from ochre to brown to deep violet.
Foliage appears in innumerable shades of green.
In all these cases the colors named are surface colors.

In a very different way, distant mountains appear uniformly blue,
no matter whether covered
with green trees or consisting of earth and rocks.
The sun is glaring white in daytime, but is full red at sunset.
The white ceilings of houses surrounded by lawns or the white-painted
eaves of a roof on a sunny day appear in bright green, which is
reflected from the grass on the ground.
All these cases present film colors.

They appear as a thin, transparent, translucent layer between the eye
and an object, independent of the object's surface color. (See plate XVII-1.)

For a very different color effect compare the coffee in a cup with the
coffee in the stem of a percolator or with the coffee in a silex glass.
It is easy to discover that, though all 3 containers hold the same
coffee, the containers show this coffee in 3 different browns:
lightest in the stem, darker in the cup, darkest in the silex glass.

In the same way, tea will look lighter in a spoon than in a cup.
Here we are dealing with volume color,
which exists and is perceived in 3-dimensional fluids.

The water of a swimming pool with blue walls will look dyed with blue
because of diffused reflection. Observing the white or blue steps
within the water, we will discover that with each step down
the blue of the water increases progressively, which presents a true
volume color effect.
In Chapter XX it will be explained in what proportion the blue increases.

On the other hand, milk remains more or less the same white,
no matter whether seen in a small or large container.
Ink and oil paint behave in a similar way.
This demonstrates that only transparent fluids present volume color.

In practice, most water colors are volume colors; several layers
on top of each other increase the darkness, weight, and intensity of a color.
Many aquarelles by Paul Klee demonstrate this.
The reverse effect of increased lightness is seen in fingerpaintings.

In contrast to water colors, such media as oil paint, gouache, and pastel
produce surface color. In most cases these paints do not change
to any extent when applied in several layers.

A new medium with volume color effect is a photosensitive glass
developed by Corning Glass Works. With increased exposure
to certain rays, the translucent opalescent white within the glass increases.
This results in a darkening of the whites with light passing through,
but in a whiter white in reflected light.

A similar effect can be achieved in tracing paper. By looking
through several layers against the light, the paper becomes darker.
However, the same layers seen from the direction of the light will appear whiter.
Since film color is not the result of physiological or psychological transformation,
it is a physical phenomenon.
Both film color and volume color might be considered tricks of nature.

XVIII Free studies— a challenge to imagination

The previous chapters deal mostly with tasks to be solved as
class problems. Through them, all class members work in 1
direction only. This means they compete for the solution of
1 given problem at a time—that of a single color effect.
Although the solutions may differ considerably, and especially so
in their presentation, the work of the whole class appears unified.

Such studies aim at the development of observation, of differentiation.
And this is particularly so through an inevitable constant comparison
going on from student to student. As a consequence, these studies
permit hardly any self-expression.

Thus, after such systematic exercises, a need for independent work arises,
and free studies are encouraged. With them one may play with colors
as one pleases, independent of exercises, independent of teachers
and of other students.

Whereas the systematic problems occupy most of the class time and
are finished afterward, the free studies are mostly homework, although
they accompany the systematic studies almost from the beginning
through the whole course.

The measure for evaluation of free studies is color relatedness.
This means color juxtaposition in which color exists for color's sake,
and therefore appears autonomous, and not merely as accompaniment
to form, to shape. (See plates XVIII-3 and XVIII-9.)

Whether something "has color" or not is as hard to define verbally as are
such questions as "what is music" or "what is musical."

The reproductions of free studies may indicate that the possibilities
are endless. Since showing such samples may present a handicap, one
might stimulate a beginning with thematic suggestions.

Experience has taught that pairs of contrasts
invoke a more distinct "meaning" and a more precise "reading."

First themes:

gay — sad   young — old   major — minor

More daring:

bright — dull   early — late   active — passive

These themes easily evoke discussions without end, since verbal reactions
to the associations with color differ vastly from person to person.

Another stimulation is the problem of free studies in colors of a limited range.
This means a restricted palette with, for instance, only contrasting
or only adjacent colors, with selections of preferred or of disliked colors.

Any of these cases may aim for concord or discord.

Such and other restrictions usually result from a personal choice.
More revealing, though harder to do, is the submission to selections
by others. To work with the preference of others, to subordinate
to someone else's palette or instrumentation, should be not only permitted
but encouraged.

All this is to promote competition. And with that comes evaluation
through comparison, which in the end means judgment.
A strong challenge to a class is to work with 3 or 4 given colors
selected by a teacher or student. This and a continued use of disliked colors
will teach that preferences and dislikes—as in life so with color
—usually result from prejudices, from lack of experience and insight.

Stripes—restricted juxtaposition

The first attempts to produce "free studies" usually result in the dominance
of form or shape—and often very pronounced—over color.

This means, in most cases, that the outlines of the colors predominate.
And, as visually the loudest, they are noticed first. Thus color appears
of secondary interest, or only as accompaniment of shape.

And this remains the normal result so long as the most decisive difference
between color in paper and color in paint is not clearly recognized:
colors in paper always consist of outspoken flat areas
which present even colors reaching precisely from edge to edge.
And the edges, by their very nature as uninterrupted endless contours,
again advocate shape first.

For this reason, it is advisable to recommend torn papers for the beginning
as they ordinarily offer looser and freer edges
than cut papers.
More experience will lead to other means of softening or hardening
color boundaries: smaller or greater contrasts of hue or of light;
elemental or complex shapes; curved, straight, broken, or dotted lines.

By combining colors exclusively in stripes—that is,
in stretched, narrow rectangles, all of the same length, varying
only in width, and touching each other in full length—
we are led to overlook their rather equal shapes and to consider them
almost shapeless.

As to placement of the stripes in horizontal or vertical direction,
the latter appears more practicable. In a left-right and
therefore sideward contact, color interaction usually
is more easily comprehensible than within an up-down connection.
And with this, our reading, connecting, grouping, and separating
of the color stripes is easier.

The first task is to organize a large number of color stripes—
all narrow, of varying width but equal length, all vertical and touching
each other, presenting only 4 colors—and only later to choose more or fewer
colors.

The aim is to find an order in which, again relatively,
all 4 colors are equally important, or, respectively, equally unimportant.
In other words, none of the colors dominates.
We say "relatively" in consideration of our individual attitude toward color,
of our differing preferences for certain colors, and our dislikes of others.

With a continuous alternation and recurrence of the 4 colors
innumerable combinations and arrangements are possible.
And the more they vary, the more they invite one to follow and to alter,
with a constant change in connecting and dividing, overlapping and intersecting
of seemingly many more than 4 colors.

We may consider such calculated juxtaposition as a symbol
of community spirit, of "live and let live," of "equal rights for all,"
of mutual respect.

We should also encourage working with very different colors,
so that light and color intensity may compete with
and balance each other.

Such studies in stripes will readily remind us of textiles,
and we may read and interpret them as fabrics of wool or cotton—
for various uses—of various color climates: from new to old, young to old,
modern to old—related to peoples, times, and periods.

The purpose is to stimulate again a reading of the meaning
of form, to invite verbal formulation of reaction to
our associations with climates in color.

The second problem in color stripes aims at different results:
dominance of 1 or more colors and broad areas is suggested;
and either coordination and / or subordination is permitted.

More freedom in the number and the choice of colors
and their extension and repetition is given.
But restrictions to equal height and vertical partitioning
remain, in order to avoid interference of form.

Whereas the first task has reminded us of striped textiles,
here one may think of walls which are subdivided for
structural, illusional, decorative purposes.

Though the second type of color studies in stripes
leads usually to a more broad and bright palette—
in a positive reaction to the first, more restricted task—
it will again prove more profitable to aim
with fewer means toward more action.

Fall leaf studies—an American discovery

Nowhere in the world, it seems to us, is the autumn foliage as brilliant
in color as in the United States.

When leaves are collected, pressed, and dried—eventually varnished,
even bleached, and sometimes also dyed or painted—they provide
a most welcome enrichment of any color paper collection.

Collected in all varieties, in all possible shades of color
—in large numbers for an easy exchange between students—they are both
exciting to see and most stimulating to work with in free studies.

As studies show, these leaves work beautifully with color paper.
They add innumerable tints and shades, with modulations and shapes
that color papers do not have. They are used singly and in groups,
in parts and combined again, repeated and reversed. Always
keep in mind the color before the shape. Colorful leaves suit all
ways of play and imagination for all kinds of order and placement.
Therefore, they remain a favorite means of study.

Naturally, leaf studies are best done in their season, in autumn,
at other times with prepared, preserved leaves which, of course,
provide more subdued, less vivid colors.

As leaf studies are free studies (usually done as homework),
they are mentioned here under that title, as are studies in stripes.
(See plates xxv-2 and xxv-6.)

XIX   The Masters— color instrumentation

It should be clear by now that our way of studying color
does not start with the past—neither with works of the past
nor with its theories.

As we begin principally with the material, color itself,
and its action and interaction as registered in our minds,
we practice first and mainly a study of ourselves.

Thus, we replace looking backward by looking first at ourselves and
our surroundings, and replace retrospection with introspection.

Though our own development and our own work are closest to us,
we see and appreciate encouragement from achievements of the past,
and gratefully pay practical respect to their originators
as often as the opportunity arises.

To honor the masters creatively is to compete with their attitude
rather than with their results, to follow an artistic understanding
of tradition—that is, to create, not to revive.

Therefore, in our study of the masters—both past and present—
there is, beyond mere retrospection and above verbal analysis,
re-creating by re-performing
their selection and presentation of color,
their seeing and reading of color—
in other words, their giving a meaning to color.

Singing a tune and playing it on instruments—
even more, conducting several instruments—
provides more contact, more insight than merely hearing the tune.
So cooking, normally and naturally, teaches more than reading recipes.

As a conclusion, we transfer paintings by masters into color paper,
in order to identify their color instrumentation. (See plate xix-1.)

Our aim is not production of precise replicas
as copyists do in museums.

We try to give a general impression only as to climate, temperature,
aroma, or sound of their work—not minute details.

The purpose of such study is neither to find out,
for instance, whether ultramarine or cobalt blue was used,
nor to register the factual content of the painter's palette.

It is another means of learning to develop
a sensitive and critical eye for color relatedness.

The result of our transformation of paintings into color paper
depends on several limitations. Naturally, in making them,
we depend on reproductions.

In 3- and 4-color halftones, all colors are represented as optical mixtures
of 3 or 4 standardized inks. These are mostly transparent,
mixing not only with each other
but also with the white paper underneath.
That is to say, such reproductions are physically already
of an absolutely different instrumentation.

The resulting false and misleading smoothness, even slickness or sweetness,
and the dramatized brightness of so-called high-key color reproduction
are easily and pleasantly counteracted and corrected by paper colors.
This is the result of the opacity or visual weight of paper colors,
and their varying density and volume.

As a rule, paintings transferred to color paper look painted;
they do not look printed.
In the case of a Van Gogh and a Soutine, we easily regain
the effect of dramatic execution.
And works of Matisse appear again as juxtaposition of flat color areas,
opaque as well as untextured.

With such studies we submit to formulations of the past
in order to provoke further comparisons
of different attitudes, temperaments, mentalities, and personalities—
all for the sake of continued self-criticism and self-evaluation.
This proclaims creative action ahead of retrospective reaction.

XX The Weber-Fechner Law— the measure in mixture

In order to obtain a graduated scale of greys, M. E. Chevreul,
the author of the famous book "The Laws of Contrast of Colour,"
gave the following instructions (from the English translation of 1868,
page 5, paragraph 11):

> Upon a sheet of cardboard divided into ten stripes,
> each about a quarter of an inch broad,
> lay a uniform tint of India ink. As soon as it is dry,
> lay a second tint on all the stripes except the first.
> As soon as the second is dry, lay a third one
> on all the stripes except the first and second,
> and so on all the rest, so as to have
> ten flat tints gradually increasing
> in depth from the first to the last.

All this sounds quite convincing, so convincing that one wonders
whether anyone has ever doubted that the result would be as promised—
whether anyone has ever followed these instructions, including M. Chevreul
himself.

All this, of course, refers to volume color (see page 45) but,
most important, it also leads to a new insight into color mixture—
after an unavoidable surprise is recognized.

The surprise is that the gradual "increase in depth" promised above
does not appear—as most people will expect—in a succession of
equal steps. Nor, when mixing pigments, does an equal gradation appear
when an equal quantity of the same color is continually added.

In this case a continued application of such layers would
unavoidably lead to such a degree of decrease that the initial increase would
disappear in a final, unsurpassable, and unchanging saturation.

Analyzing Chevreul's method of applying one layer on top of another,
one recognizes not only an additive mixture with regard to color, but
also a subtractive mixture with regard to light.

More precisely, this demonstrates an arithmetical progression
in both directions—and both are physical progressions only.

In the diagrams on page 56, this physical fact is presented
by a row of rising steps of equal height and width, the movement of which
follows a straight line.

As said before, and clearly shown in Klee's water colors, the rate of
increase gradually decreases. Therefore, the rise of the steps will be
less and less high. Consequently, the physically straight line of
direction becomes psychologically a curve, ending in a horizontal line
representing saturation, which ends both increase and decrease.

This leads to the question: what is necessary to produce a visually
even progression in mixture?

The answer was found by Weber (Wilhelm Eduard, 1804–91) and Fechner
(Gustav Theodor, 1801–87). It is formulated in the so-called Weber-Fechner Law:
The visual perception of an arithmetical progression depends upon a physical
geometric progression.

Explained in diagrams shown on the next page, this means:
If the first 2 steps measure 1 and 2 units in rise, then
 step 3 is not only 1 unit more (that is, 3 in an arithmetical proportion),
but is twice as much (that is, 4 in a geometric
proportion). The successive steps then measure 8, 16, 32, 64 units.
Such increases describe an upward curve ending in a straight vertical line, meaning,
again, saturation.

However, the reading of such geometric increase will describe a straight line
in our mind. We think and "feel" that we read steps of equal height.

To demonstrate this surprising discrepancy between physical fact and psychic effect,
and, more important, to become convinced of it through one's own experience,
the following exercise is recommended:

On a white paper, layers of very light transparent coats of a very thin color
are placed on top of each other; first, as M. Chevreul suggests,
in an arithmetical progression (1, 2, 3, 4, 5, etc. layers); then, in a
second row, in a geometric progression (1, 2, 4, 8, 16, etc. layers),
on the same paper. In both rows, contiguous steps of equal width are required.

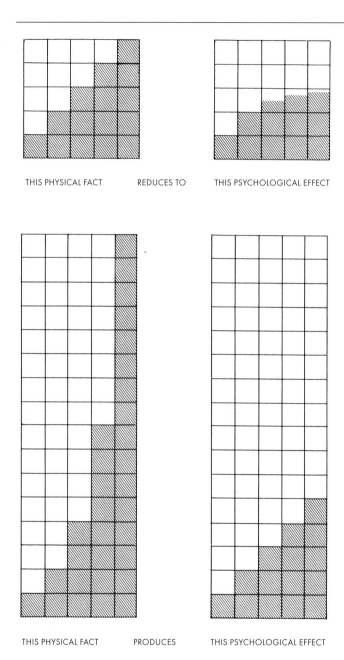

THIS PHYSICAL FACT   REDUCES TO   THIS PSYCHOLOGICAL EFFECT

THIS PHYSICAL FACT   PRODUCES   THIS PSYCHOLOGICAL EFFECT

For accurate comparison of the 2 rows—of arithmetical and geometric increases—
precision is necessary. For this reason, water color should be avoided,
because it rarely provides even coats and always ends not only
in heavy but in unevenly heavy contours. Most advisable is the use of
film-like acetate sheets of the thinnest tints available, with adhesive backs
which provide the advantages of easy montage and invisible paste.
There are several makes, such as "Zip-a-tone," "Artype," and "Cello-tak."

In case these are not available, very thin translucent paper (waxed sandwich paper)
might demonstrate—in transparence—the 2 different effects,
when observed against light.

For another demonstration in turbid means—in reflected light—
layers of thinnest whites on black paper will provide proof in an opposite direction—
the very different effects of arithmetical and geometric increase or decrease.

These studies also teach that the "decreasing increase" can be seen in the boundaries
separating the steps: In an arithmetical order of contiguous mixtures,
the boundaries gradually become softer, whereas in a geometric order the boundaries
remain equally distinct.

Such studies, of course, are only theoretically true. Because of slight material
imprecisions, the studies show occasional aberrations from the rule.

Though the Weber-Fechner Law enables "equal stepping up" (in light and in dark,
within specific hues), it is deflected by the relativity of color.

In steps which are not much wider than they are deep, these steps visually do not
remain horizontal or on an even level, as in the diagram on page 58, left.

In steps which are broader, a "fluting" effect occurs, reminiscent of the
channeling of Doric columns, as in the diagram on page 58, right.

A convincing outdoor demonstration of the Weber-Fechner Law is presented
in swimming pools painted, for example, blue. Because of reflection, the
water appears thinly tinted blue. Visually following the steps downward,
one easily recognizes an increase of blueness. Since the steps are
equally deep, equal amounts of blueness are added. This
arithmetical physical proportion is again perceived in a decreasing geometric proportion.

When the edges of the steps are compared in a downward direction they appear
gradually softer. There is a double reason for this effect: First, as the increase
of blueness simultaneously reduces light, the defining edges of the steps
appear less clear. Second, as the increase in blueness also decreases,
the contrast between neighboring blues is reduced.
Consequently, the separation of the edges of the steps becomes
less distinct. Both reasons follow the Weber-Fechner Law and are unrelated
to any law of light refraction. Although light refraction also causes
illusion in visual perception, it presents an entirely different principle
because it is concerned with an optical effect. The Weber-Fechner Law
explains a perceptual phenomenon.

It is surprising and unfortunate that the Weber-Fechner Law is almost
unknown among colorists. Its importance is more recognized in physics—in astronomy,
electricity, and acoustics. It also proves to be important in psychology—in the perception
of sound, weight, temperature—as well as in the perception of light and color.
(See plate xx-1.)
The presentation below of the important Weber-Fechner discovery was simplified visually
and verbally for an easier understanding, but it should be emphasized that all Weber-
Fechner calculations are done in logarithmic progressions which theoretically do not reach
saturation points.

ACTUALLY PERCEIVED

XXI From color temperature to humidity in color

Earlier, when explaining light intensity as lightness and color intensity as brightness, we found that agreement is easier in the first case, and difficult in the second.

This is because, in defining such qualities, we deal on the one side with physical facts and on the other with perceptual reactions which permit either a factual measure or an interpretation of illusions. As a result, there are in the latter case various views and opinions, and different, if not contradictory, readings.

Any measuring of light-dark qualities is not unrelated to a scaling of light-heavy relationships. Light-dark and light-heavy lead easily to soft-hard comparisons; or, quick-slow and early-late connect with young-old, and with warm-cool, as well as with wet-dry.

Such and other chain connections have led even to such opposites as here and there, indicating spatial differentiation.

The 2 most comprehensive of the above polarities in color are first, light-dark and light-heavy, and second, the temperature contrast warm-cool.

In defining the placement of such contrasts within color circles, we will see, besides their uneven distribution and their so-called neutrals separating them, their slight overlappings of each other when we compare one circle with the other. (See diagrams, next page.)

As to warm and cool, it is accepted in Western tradition that normally blue appears cool and that the adjacent group, yellow-orange-red, looks warm. As any temperature can be read higher or lower in comparison with other temperatures, these qualifications are only relative. Therefore, there are also warm blues and cool reds possible within their own hues.

But when these temperature indicators, red and blue, are combined with color neutrals, as whites, blacks, and greys, and with their mixtures, particularly in mixtures with the temperature neutrals green and violet, then personal interpretations of temperatures may easily become disparate.

Therefore, it will be comprehensible that such theories of interpretation may lead to and end in personal beliefs. So it is not surprising that the warm-cool principle in color which successfully dominated the Munich school of painting around the turn of the century resulted finally in fruitless controversies.

It was successful in gaining followers by offering a theory for defining spatial relationship of colors, through their higher and lower illusional temperature. As this warm-cool relationship was closely connected with the light-dark contrast, the hardest but apparently lasting conversion then was that light was cold and shadows warm, at least outdoors. It split up in factions of different beliefs about the function of cool and warm with regard to spatial directions in painting, whether the <u>here</u> contra <u>there</u> was decisive, or the <u>above</u> contra <u>below</u>, or the <u>in</u> contra <u>out</u>. A clear example of these opposites is the contrast between Boucher's receding deepening with vermilion red, and Rubens' advancing heightening with white.

All this may be a reason why the warm-cool contrast is not in fashion today, although a new theory declares warm near and cool far, because the former is of longer and the latter of shorter wave length, and they are, therefore, optically registered in different ways. But optical and perceptual registration are not necessarily parallel. (See plate XXI-1.)

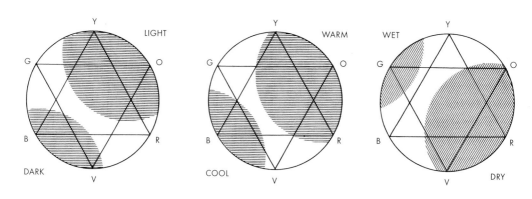

XXII Vibrating boundaries— enforced contours

As a deception, this effect is related to our earlier experience
in which 2 colors appeared as 3 or 4 colors.

However, the additional illusionary colors
often are hard to define as to their hue.

They often appear as shadow on one side of the boundary
and as light reflected on the other side.

Or sometimes this vibration presents just a duplication
or triplication of the boundary line.

The conditions for these varying effects occur between colors
which are contrasting in their hues but also close or similar
in light intensity.

Though this effect refers to the after-image,
its physio-psychological function apparently
seems not to have been clarified.

Often, under the same conditions, it is perceived by some people
and not by others.

It is visible and not visible with or without glasses;
or, similarly, with interchanging of near and far focus.

This initially exciting effect also feels aggressive
and often even uncomfortable to our eyes.
One finds it rarely used except for a screaming effect
in advertising, and as a result it is unpleasant, disliked, and avoided.
(See plates XXII-1 and XXII-2.)

XXIII Equal light intensity—
vanishing boundaries

Though rarely perceived, it is a fact that articulate boundaries
between colors can be made nearly unrecognizable, or made practically
invisible—through the choice of color alone.

This very surprising and most exciting of all color phenomena depends,
like all other effects, on specific conditions.

The effect is the opposite of the aforementioned vibrating boundaries,
and it is not possible between very contrasting hues.
It is confined to adjacent, neighboring colors and depends most decisively
on equal "light intensity." Only real equality in lightness
or an equivalent real equality in darkness produces the effect here aimed at
and searched for.

Now, since the term "equal value" has unfortunately been misused too often
for colors lacking just this quality, incompetent judgment has distorted
this term to a falsified measure. In this way, "equal values"
are more spoken about than realized—than actually seen.

Thus, we can safely state that very few people—including many colorists
and painters—have ever seen 2 adjacent colors
of true equal light value—that is, of exact equality in light,
of the same level of light, or, in a sense, the same altitude of light.

This will indicate that equal light intensity presents,
besides a most challenging exercise, a most difficult task
demanding most of all—patience.

Because several of our color classes were not able to present
even 1 convincing color couple of equal light intensity,
this makes it an exercise for teachers willing to demonstrate
that in all teaching the personal example is the strongest incentive.

Earlier, right after the test "Which is the lighter and / or darker?"
we had the opportunity to prepare for this difficult exercise,
which usually is the last exercise of our course.

When we were collecting pairs of colors hard to distinguish as lighter or darker
we were often tempted to
consider some of them to be of "equal value."

At that time we learned that in cases difficult to decide upon,
which we named "near-equal light intensities," or "almost-equals,"
the after-image test can be a helpful measure. (See diagram, page 13.)

Though sometimes it may appear hopeless to find equal light intensities in paint
and painting, in color papers, or in our surroundings, we have found that
nature occasionally provides an opportunity to see them on cumulus clouds
against blue sky.

When these clouds, often lined up in horizontal groups,
appear gleaming white in their upper part in full sunlight,
separated from and rising against a distant deep blue,
then underneath they show grey tones as shaded white.
These shades merge, or even hinge, with the same
but here very close blue. Why very close? This grey is
of the same light intensity as the neighboring blue below.
Thus, the boundaries between grey and blue vanish,
and we do not see where clouds end and where sky begins.
With such clouds, this is best observed with the sun at our backs.

In order to produce this provocative color effect—but also the most
delicate one—all disturbing effects of paper (such as different surfaces)
and of montage (visible edges or paste marks) must be carefully avoided.
(See plate XXIII-2.)

Therefore, the 2 papers of equal light intensity must be mounted as
inlay (known as "intarsia").

In this process the papers are placed within each other, instead of on top of
each other. Thus the thickness of the paper does not show, and, more important,
its very disturbing shadows are eliminated—provided the papers are of
equal thickness.

For precision fitting, so that the joints will not show, the papers to be inlaid are formed simultaneously in a single cutting.

The finer the knife (best, the thinnest razor blade), the thinner the paper, and the harder the ground to cut on (preferably glass), the better the fitting will be and the less the joints will show. It is also essential that no glue seep in to mark the joints.

As the selection of the papers here demands patience, so their presentation demands skill and cleanliness.

XXIV Color theories—color systems

Originally, we began our color course with a presentation
of various color systems, of color theories.

With the discovery that color is the most relative medium in art, and that
its greatest excitement lies beyond rules and canons,
a more sensitive discrimination was needed.

The more a creative use of color developed, the less desirable became
a merely trustful and obedient application.

A sensitive eye for color became our first concern.

As a result, we came to present color systems not at the beginning
but at the end of our course.

We learned that their often beautiful order is more recognized and
appreciated when eyes and minds are—after productive exercises—
better prepared and more receptive.
In a laboratory course as described, it is not the ambition
to provide a comprehensive knowledge of many theories.
We can introduce only briefly the most important systems, which are
systematic groupings of the colors of the visible sun spectrum,
presented in 2-dimensional or 3-dimensional order.
However, we encourage extended interest in private study of theories.

In presenting systems showing organized color relationship,
we usually start with the rarely published equilateral triangle
subdivided into 9 equilateral triangles, shown on page 66.
(See also plate XXIV-1.)

We then refer to Schopenhauer's experiment on the relation and balance
of light with quantity within the color wheel, as explained on page 43.

Of the contemporary systems, we present and analyze briefly the order
of the Munsell Color Tree, as well as the Ostwald Color System,
and show an offspring of the latter, the Faber Birren Color System.

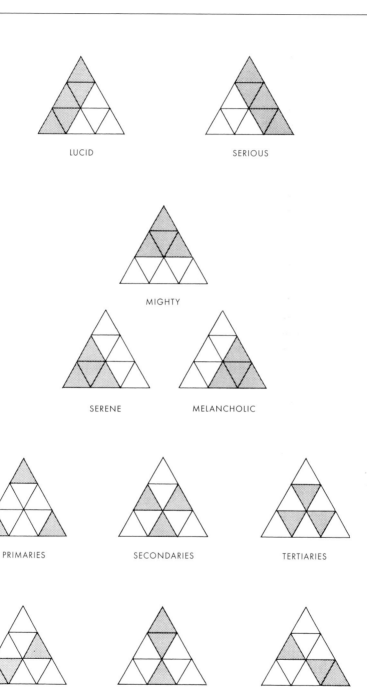

LUCID

SERIOUS

MIGHTY

SERENE

MELANCHOLIC

PRIMARIES

SECONDARIES

TERTIARIES

COMPLEMENTARIES WITH THEIR MIXTURES WHICH ARE DOMINATED BY THEIR PRIMARIES

Besides the difference in measurements within these systems,
we point out their practical value for industrial uses.

We also show the limitations of the systems,
particularly in connection with painting.
Only the Munsell System presents a calculation of color quantity
with regard to area extension, without counting an additional
effect through recurrence.

We emphasize that color harmonies, usually the special interest
or aim of color systems, are not the only desirable relationship.
As with tones in music, so with color—dissonance is as desirable
as its opposite, consonance.
After such brief introduction to established color systems
we introduce a more recent, most important development,
the spectrophotometer, for automatic color analysis.

Since no purpose is served by going into further details of color systems,
it seems worth while to distinguish 3 basically different approaches
to color based upon the different interests of
the physicist, the psychologist, and the colorist.
To indicate only a single difference: whereas the primary colors
for the colorist (painters, designers) are, as we know, yellow-red-blue,
the physicist has 3 other primaries (not including yellow),
and the psychologist counts 4 primaries (the fourth being green),
plus 2 neutrals, white and black.

XXV On teaching color— some color terms

In the previous chapters we have presented a studio course,
or, if you prefer, a laboratory or workshop course
which opposes an administrative attitude of "theory and practice."
Naturally, practice is not preceded but followed by theory.
Such study promotes a more lasting teaching and learning
through experience. Its aim is development of creativeness
realized in discovery and invention—the criteria of creativity,
or flexibility, being imagination and fantasy. Altogether
it promotes "thinking in situations," a new educational concept
unfortunately little known and less cultivated, so far.

We have described, up to now, the basic color problems to be solved,
and have presented them in a logical sequence in which each problem
prepares for following ones.

The color plates selected for reproduction in this edition are strictly studies,
that is, experimental tryouts. They aim at 1 distinct effect only, which,
at the time, was given as an exercise, obligatory for all members of the class.
These exercises are not meant to illustrate, or to decorate or beautify
something, but aim at the development of the ability to produce the
desired color effects. This reiterates our disbelief in self-expression, either
as a way of study or as its aim, in schools.

After too much non-teaching, non-learning, and a consequent non-seeing,
—in too many art "activities"—it is time to advocate again a basic
step-by-step learning which promotes recognition of insight coming
from experience, and evaluation resulting from comparison.
This, in sum, means recognition of development and improvement,
that is, of growth, growth of ability. This growth is not only
a most exciting experience; it is inspiring and thus
the strongest incentive for intensified action, for continued investigation
(search instead of re-search), for learning through conscious practice.

Gestalt psychology has proved that 3-dimensionality is perceived earlier and more easily than 2-dimensionality. This explains why children do not begin—as most art teachers still wish—with painting and drawing, which are lateral abstractions on a 2-dimensional plane, but begin all by themselves with building, constructing in space, on a ground and upward, in 3 dimensions.

We believe that art education is an essential part of general education, including so-called higher learning. We promote, therefore, after a natural and easy laissez-faire as an initial challenge, an early shift from aimless play to directed study and work, which offers, with a basic training, a continuous excitement of growth.

To say this in psychological-educational terms, it means a shift from a recognition of the first but primitive drive for being occupied, entertained—Beschäftigungstrieb— to a more advanced drive, or better, need, for being productive, creative—Gestaltungstrieb.

The results of our trial-and-error experimentation, mostly done after class, are exhibited at the beginning of the next class. (These studies we call the "admission tickets" to the class.)

They are then compared and evaluated by the entire class, students and teacher. First, every class member makes his selection and compares his preferences with his own contributions. Then, we —that is, the teacher or a student or students—select the best examples of "psychological engineering." This qualification we confer on a convincing presentation because it eliminates misleading reading of the study's purpose and its desired effect.

The normal procedure in presenting a new problem often is to show a sample exercise and to point to its specific effect. The class is then asked to produce equal effects with similar and other colors—without first being told how to do it.

After a while, a collection of the first trials—wrong as well as "on the way" or right—will give an opportunity to lead, to direct, to point at (or to indicate only by comparison forth and back) new ways of promising investigation.

It comes as a pleasant surprise in a step-by-step learning that the further the course proceeds, the more each succeeding problem is accidentally if not actually presented among the studies shown at the beginning of a class. The teacher may prefer to present the new problem with this "step ahead" (thus evading his own prepared presentation), as a new direction emanating from the class. This "step ahead" will prove a most contagious stimulus to the class.

As basic rules of any language must be practiced continuously, and therefore are never fixed, so exercises toward distinct color effects never are done or over. New and different cases will be discovered time and again, and should be presented to the class again and again. In this way the study will be a mutual give and take. It will also show that all thorough study is basic, and that all education is self-education. This indicates that we expect from every student several solutions to each problem.

In the end, teaching is a matter not of method but of heart. Therefore, the most decisive factor is the teacher's personality. His enthusiastic concern with the student's growth counts more than how much he knows. It is well known that "the teacher is always right," but rarely does this fact elicit respect or sympathy; even less often does it prove competence and authority.

But the teacher actually is right and always will gain confidence when he admits that he does not know, that he cannot decide, and, as it often is with color, that he is unable to make a choice or to give advice.

Besides, good teaching is more a giving of right questions than a giving of right answers.

A few color terms which need additional explanation

Relativity:
The length of any object is relative to the length
of longer or shorter objects. Thus, any in-between length, seen in 2 different relationships, presents 2 different values. Therefore, changing measure results in changing evaluations.

In a similar way, as we learned before, 1 temperature can feel as 2. Also, weight may be registered in different ways. If, of 3 hands, the first holds only a small sheet of paper, the second a pile of sheets or a book, and the third a pile of books, then physically each of the 3 hands is exposed to weight. The first will feel nothing or only a soft touch, the second clearly some pressure downward, and the third may even feel pain.

Relativity is caused by a variance of measure, by lack or avoidance of standard rules, or by changing viewpoints. As a result, 1 phenomenon has varying views, readings, and different meanings.

This instability of value is extremely characteristic of color. Resulting from the after-image, a light grey, for instance, may look dark at one time and almost white at another, and at various times like a shade or a tint of any color, as green may look reddish.

The purpose of most of our color studies is to prove that color is the most relative medium in art, that we almost never perceive what color is physically.

The mutual influencing of colors we call—interaction. Seen from the opposite viewpoint, it is—interdependence.

Though we were taught, only a few years ago, that there is no connection whatever between visual and auditory perception, we know now that a color changes visually when a changing tone is heard simultaneously. This, of course, makes the relativity of color still more obvious, just as tongue and eye perceptions interdepend when colors of food and of its containers increase or diminish our appetite.

Factual—Actual:
In dealing with color relativity or color illusion, it is practical to distinguish factual facts from actual facts.

The data on wave length—the result of optical analysis of light spectra— we acknowledge as fact.

This is a factual fact.

It means something remaining what it is, something probably not undergoing changes.

But when we see opaque color as transparent or perceive opacity as translucence, then the optical reception in our eye has changed in our mind to something different. The same is true when we see 3 colors as 4 or as 2, or 4 colors as 3, when we see flat, even colors as intersecting colors and their fluting effect, or when we see distinct 1-contour boundaries doubled or vibrating or just vanishing.

These effects we call actual facts.

This kind of fact seems parallel to the common saying, "what actually happened," that is, what happened in time, what went on, what moved, what developed.

But "actual size" usually means something fixed, something remaining permanent, standing still. Therefore, "factual size" would be more truthful because "actual" is related to "action." It is something not fixed, but changing with time.

"Action" is the noun for the verb "to act." Acting in visual presentation is to change by giving up, by losing identity. When we act, we change appearance and behavior, we act as someone else.

For further clarification, therefore, actors who present only themselves remain always the same. They may appear interesting, but they do not act. In our terms they remain factual. However, when an actor is able to appear as Henry VIII, so that we overlook or forget who he factually is, and when he also can be expected to play Henry IX or Henry X, then he is a real actor, able to give up his own identity and present someone else's appearance and personality.

Color acts in a similar way. Because of the after-image (the simultaneous contrast), colors influence and change each other forth and back. They continuously interact—in our perception.

Value:
The word as such, when unspecified, permits application in innumerable directions. By itself, it does not reveal on what level, in what direction or field evaluation is meant.

In color, it is a distinct measure only in connection with the Munsell System. There, Munsell defines value as the lightness of a color. In connection with other systems it has no outspoken meaning. The French word <u>valeur</u> has a broader meaning. Unfortunately, the careless use of "value," particularly with regard to equal lightness—as well as false examples reproduced in books—has destroyed it as a means of measure. Therefore we use "light intensity" instead as a self-explanatory term. (See Chapters v, page 12, and xxiii, page 62.)

Variants versus variety

The word "variety," although recently a favored design term, has become discredited because of increased abuse. It has become a pretentious recommendation for designs of questionable merit. It is applied to protect hurried changes, to excuse poor alterations, or to defend any accidental and meaningless whim. It even appears as a weapon to prevent rejection, to force credits. Thus the excuse "for variety's sake" remains a warning signal.

To replace this negative criterion, we are in favor of a related word of better reputation, the design term "variant." As variety usually concerns changes of details, variant means a more thorough re-doing of a whole or of a part within a given scheme. Although variant may remind us slightly of imitative plagiarism, normally it results from a thorough study. Because of a more comprehensive comparison forth and back, it usually aims at a new presentation. On the whole, variants demonstrate, besides a sincere attitude, a healthy belief that there is no final solution in form; thus form demands unending performance and invites constant reconsideration—visually as well as verbally.

XXVI In lieu of a bibliography— my first collaborators

This book presents results of search, not of what is academically called research.

As it is not a compilation from books, it does not end with a list of books—either books read, or books not read.

Instead, this book ends with an acknowledgment of my students who are the authors of the sample studies, and whom I therefore consider my indirect but first collaborators.

In addition to the dedication of this book, I should like to state that my students in color have taught me more color than have books about color.

Many students of this color course (which has been developed in the United States) not only have found solutions of their own to known problems, but also have visualized and discovered new problems, new solutions, and new presentations. Although rarely shown, and therefore barely known so far, their contributions deserve publication in the interest of a new intensified training of eyes and minds—in both art education and general education.

Those contributions come from 2 sides, from a majority of normally gifted students, as well as from the minority of more gifted students. And particularly this majority has taught me how to proceed, how to open eyes and minds; even more important, it has taught me what not to do.

We should have liked to name here the authors of all the sample studies reproduced in the first edition. Unfortunately, many names are lacking, uncertain, or lost. The known names are listed alphabetically in the original edition, followed by the numbers of the folders containing their studies.

Plates and commentary

A color has many faces—the relativity of color

IV-1   A color has many faces, and 1 color can be made to appear as 2 different
colors. In the original design for the study IV-1, horizontal dark blue and yellow stripes
were on a flap which could be lifted to show that a vertical stripe of ochre
is the same color at the top as at the bottom.

Here it is almost unbelievable that the upper small and the lower
small squares are part of the same paper strip and therefore are the
same color.

And no normal human eye is able to see both squares—alike.

Note: Plate numbers correspond to Folder numbers in the original edition.

IV-3   Why is the green presented as a grill?
        Or, what is the perceptual reason for it?

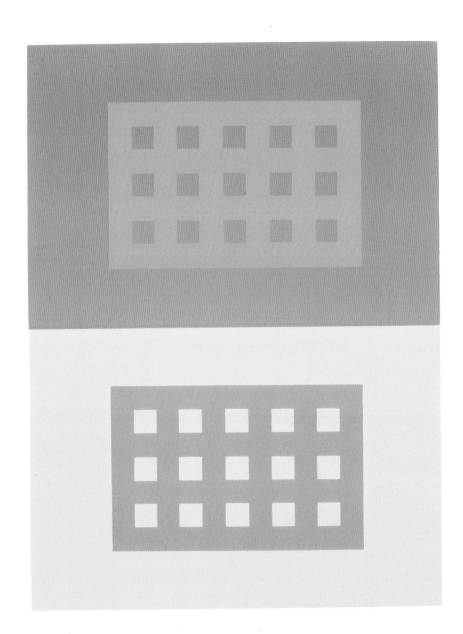

IV-4   The inner smaller violets are
        factually alike.
        But the upper one appears to refer to
        the outer lighter violet at the bottom.

Gradation studies
CHAPTER V

V-1 The gradation in plate v-1 is a collage of small snippets of greys carefully collected from magazine illustrations, which should come from the same publications to ensure the same hue of the black.

They are arranged downward in the softest possible transition from deep black to clear white, and then mounted as 4 equal-sized rectangles on a cardboard sheet of a correct middle grey so that they appear as in a window frame with a central cross, of which all parts are the same width.

This combination of decreasing blacks into clear whites within an unchanging framework results in the following interaction: the 3 verticals of the frame appear increasingly lighter toward the top, and similarly darker toward the base.

Of the 3 horizontals within that frame the upper appears lighter, and the lowest one darker. And the middle horizontal almost vanishes from merging with its neighboring middle-grey snippets.

Although such study depends very much on precision and patience, similar studies should be encouraged. It should be mentioned that samples of a real middle grey are hardest to find.

V-2   These 2 advertisements, each showing a perfume bottle
against the ground of a black-white gradation, are
partly overpasted with 1 and with 3 vertical bands which show
a second gradation reversing the ground.
But this second gradation exists only in our perception.
In fact, the vertical bands consist solely of an
entirely even middle grey which turns unrecognizable
through a light illusion.

V-3   For the study of color intensity or brightness, we selected
       from 8 tints, shades, or tones the 1 most typical for each hue,
       and presented it as such through an emphasis on placement.
       For a "fair" comparison, all samples appear
       in the same amount and the same shape. As stated before,
       personal preferences and prejudices will result in diverging
       votes, or selections. (See Text, pages 16–17.)

       The choice of the bluest blue, marked by its vertical and
       raised placement, will easily find agreement.

       Disagreement must be expected with the 8 reds. Surely both reds at the left
       will get votes of first choice, the first one probably
       from older, and the second one from younger voters. The second,
       a vermilion or orange-red, has become fashionable with designers,
       especially typographers, in black and red advertising on white.

Reversed grounds
CHAPTER VI

VI-3   Hold the plate with the yellow rectangle on the left. We see here
2 rectangles of 2 different colors connected as a pair.
Within the pairs are 2 X-like forms which look different.

The longer we observe the X's, and the more we compare them
(best at some distance), the more we see that each
repeats the color of the opposite, neighboring ground.
We perceive the whole (both studies together) in 2 colors
of which each appears 2 times, namely as ground and as figure.

We do not see
that the whole consists of more than 2 colors, and that the X's
are alike—meaning of one and the same color—
and therefore different from the colors of both grounds.

Consequently, we do not see that the
study consists not of 2 colors, but of 3.

This is made visible
only through the small horizontal connection between the X's.

This demonstrates
a discrepancy between factual colors of the X's and
the visual perception of these colors. In other words, we do not see
what these colors physically are.

We study this
first, not as a surprising or entertaining illusion but to make
eyes and mind aware of the wonders of color interaction; second,
to learn to utilize color deception in creative color performance.

The problem is:
Find that color which on 2 different grounds loses its identity.
The question is:
What color relatedness makes 3 colors look like 2?

VI-4   3 colors appear as 2.

On brown and violet grounds, the center squares look like
the grounds exchanged, violet and brown. But they are of the
same color, precisely alike, and at the same time refer to
the neighboring grounds. The true color of the 2
central squares therefore becomes unrecognizable, as it loses
its identity.

VI-4 The semicircular forms appear as different colors above and below,
and these refer to the reciprocal grounds.
The visible connection between the 2 groups
reveals that they are of the same color, therefore alike.
Question: Which color produces such deception?
And notice how the half-rings lead us to compare them with
"the other side." This study therefore presents an example of
"psychological engineering."

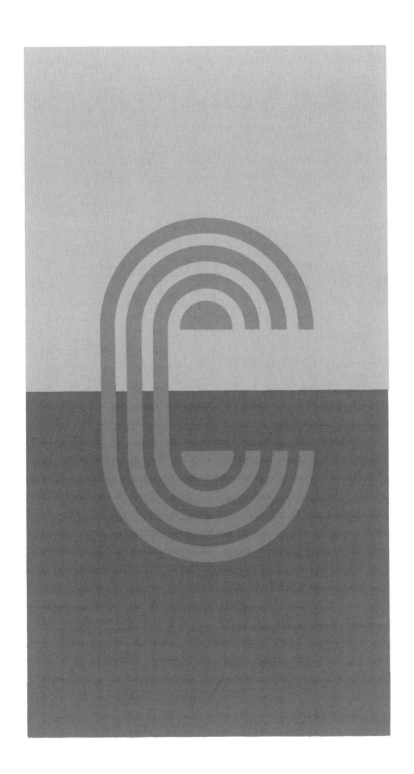

Subtraction of color
CHAPTER VII

A new task: 2 different colors are to look alike,
or 4 colors are to look like 3, as explained on page 20 of the Text.
We consider this color change as color subtraction.

In order to present these unusual and little-known effects appropriately,
first cover the 2 colors in the margins or peripheries of the studies.
Then compare the centered small rectangles and find out
how equal or how similar they look.

For the best simultaneous comparison do not look from one center to
the other but focus firmly on a point in the middle between them,
which will be within the boundary of the grounds.

Now, after the likeness or similarity has been recognized in the centers,
uncover the small color blocks in the margins (noted above), and see
what they really are. These 2 colors were the point of departure
for the study.

VII-2   A solution in heavy color.

VII-4   Hold plate VII-4 with the deep green ground on the left, and the light grey ground on the right.

Below them are 2 contiguous horizontal stripes, the upper one a brownish-green on top of a thin ochreous yellow.

The small rectangles in the centers of the large rectangles seem to be alike.

We see 1 pair of larger upright rectangles and 2 pairs of smaller
horizontal rectangles, each pair connected along a vertical axis.
The 2 upper pairs carry narrow stripes, on the larger as diagonals,
and on the smaller connected in a central horizontal axis.

As to color, the deep red and yellowish off-white grounds at top
are reversed in the second pair. The quite different lower pair
contains a clear contrast, Naples yellow and ochre.

When comparing the 2 diagonals simultaneously, that is, not in sequence
but focusing on the middle between them, they will appear
very similar or even alike. But they are precisely
the same as the horizontal stripes beneath them, and
therefore factually as different as the colors at the bottom,
which are ochre and Naples yellow.

Reading the study in the opposite direction—upward—the quite different
Naples yellow and ochre, when seen reversed on the contrasting grounds
of the middle pair, appear even more different. But when shown
in the same order on the reversed colors of the upper grounds,
they change from a distinct contrast to a pair of similar colors.
Naples yellow and ochre are changed to look alike.

VII-7 Hold the plate with the 3 small rectangles at the right.
This study shows a very courageous solution to the problem
because it makes a very light grey and a dark, almost black-grey
appear alike.

Of the 3 small rectangles, the 2 lighter ones (above each other)
are exactly alike, and look exactly alike since they are seen
on the same ground, white.

The third small and connected rectangle—because of its darkness—
appears in color similar or equal to the large dark ground
at the left. Thus, it seems unbelievable that the small dark one
is precisely repeated in the center of the dark ground where it
looks much lighter—unbelievably lighter.

Now, having next to each other dark on darker and light on lighter—
the left and right center as horizontal neighbors
in parallel optical conditions (equal placement, shape, and
quantity relationship)—we are able to compare them. If this is done
properly, which means simultaneously (not alternatingly,
as explained before), we will perceive that the white-grey
and the black-grey, seen first as connected contrasts, appear alike.
Q. E. D., what was to be proved.

For a visual proof, make a flap by tracing the 2 dark-grey rectangles
on a sheet of paper from your school notebook
(usually slightly translucent), cut them out, somewhat smaller,
and compare what you see through these openings.

After-image
CHAPTER VIII

VIII-1 Turn the page so that the red circle is on the left.
If we stare for half a minute at the red circle, focusing continually
on the marked center, and then focus on the white center,
we do not see white. The color we see there
is the after-image of red and is a simultaneous contrast.

VIII-2   For a clear understanding of interaction of color caused by
interdependence of color we should experience what "after-image"
means. Before going on to study plate VIII-2 complete the exercise
described on page 22.

Now hold the plate with the white square on the right. On the left are yellow
circles of equal diameter which touch each other and fill out a white
square. There is a black dot in its center. On the right is an empty
white square, also with a centered black dot. Each is on a black ground.
After staring for half a minute at the left square, shift the focus suddenly
to the right square.

Here one experiences a very different after-image. Instead of seeing the
complement of the yellow circles (blue), diamond shapes are seen—
the leftover shapes of the circles—in yellow. This illusion is a double
and thus reversed after-image, sometimes called contrast reversal.

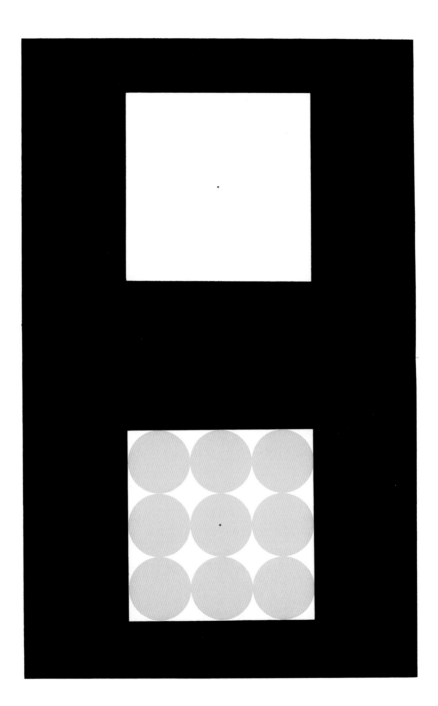

Color mixture in paper
CHAPTER IX

IX-1 In painting it is easy to mix pigments by pouring them together and stirring them, which achieves an in-between color as a mixture. Since this is not possible with paper, we must imagine a possible "in-between color." In plate IX-1 we superimpose part of a brown rectangle on a rosy-red rectangle. First we pass our eyes from left to right several times across the overlapping area, in which the mixture should appear.

After several passages back and forth we see that the red appears to come through the brown at the left, and the brown seems to come through the red at the right border of the overlap. This is proof that we have a true mixture.

It is easy to see that the right edge of the brown rectangle has a heavier boundary than the left edge of the red. Therefore this mixture contains more brown than red. Thus, the brown is on top; in other words, the brown is dominant in the mixture.

Now try to find a mixture in which the red is on top and therefore dominant.

Read Chapter XI and find some color mixture in paper that produces various space illusions.

IX-3 Even texture effects submit to the illusion of transparence.
(l.) A saturated middle blue and a typical chocolate brown are
overlapped by the same beige-like tone decorated with simulated
leather texture. Within the overlappings appear illusionary
mixtures of a tint of blue and of brown, and with these an
illusion of transparence. We also see the textural leather
décor carried over, making the transparence still more convincing.
We are easily reminded of those thin, light, dyed, and inexpensive
plastics which are made to cover lightweight luggage.

(r.) A rectangle of newspaper chosen for its texture of letters
(which we call typofacture) is overlapped by (or overlapping?)
a square of an even deep yellow. Here the overlapping shows
illusions of mixture and transparence. It also preserves the
precise size, type, and spacing of the letters.

The question is: How is the illusion of transparence
or translucence achieved?
A second question: How would it be possible to achieve
a transparence illusion in which the newspaper appears on
top of the yellow paper?

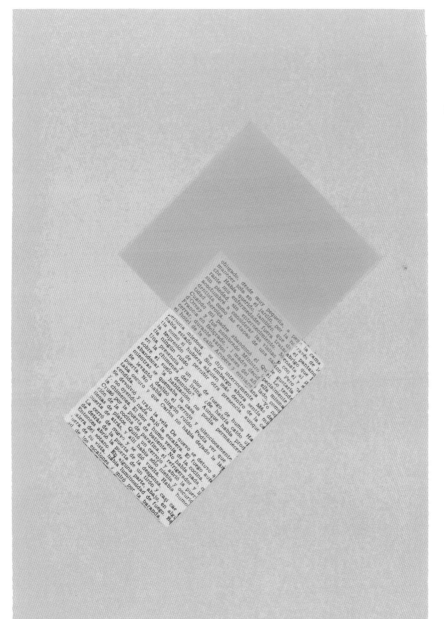

Additive and subtractive mixture
CHAPTER X

X-1   Hold plate x-1 with the dark background on the left.
       Obviously both studies are based on the same underlying design
       of 3 overlapping rectangles, providing a common subdivision of area.

       The 3 rectangles are of equal shape and size,
       and hinged in their combined left corners. They are, furthermore,
       related as tints of the same color, namely a grey-violet.

       With regard to light, the 2 groups of rectangles move
       in opposite directions. At left, from a dark ground to a light center,
       at right from a light ground to a dark center.

       On both sides, each of the 3 rectangles overlaps the 2 others
       only once. By looking transparent (in fact, they are opaque)
       they produce in our perception illusions of mixture, in 3 steps
       of either light or shade—a gradual increase in light at the left
       but a decrease in light at the right.

       With their contrasting results of gaining and of losing light,
       these studies explain a basic difference in mixture,
       that is, mixture in direct color—which is light—and its opposite,
       mixture in reflected color—produced by pigment.

       The first, the product of a mixture by a physicist,
       by combining light (direct color) results in addition of light.
       Whereas the second, a combining of pigments (indirect, reflected color)
       and done by the colorist, results in subtraction of light.

       Now, since both studies are done in pigments (inks),
       they "present," in fact, reflected light only;
       they also "represent," in illusion only,
       at right, subtractive mixture, the area of the painter,
       and at left, additive mixture, the realm of the physicist.

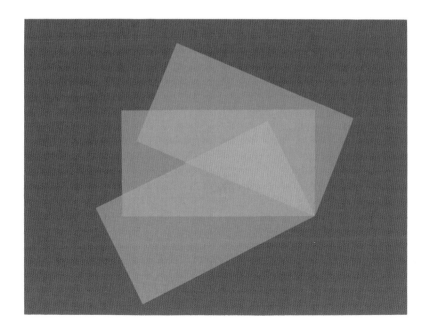

Transparence and space-illusion
CHAPTER XI

XI-1   This deserves recognition as an unusually precise study
        of a mixture of 2 colors in a gradation of 9 equidistant steps of red—
        equidistant by their proper increase of yellow content.
        It presents itself most actively when seen with the little dot
        in the upper left corner. Then the gradual upward increase in light
        reads more decisively than the equally precise
        increase in red in the opposite direction.

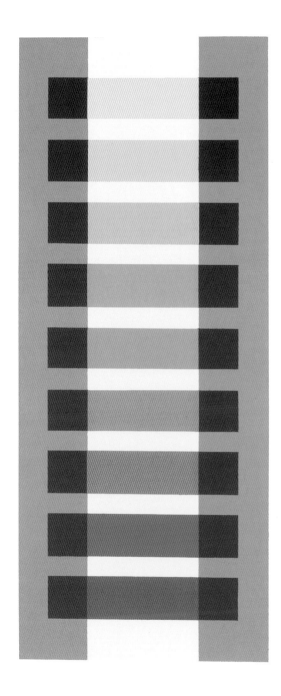

XI-2   A presentation of a blue and a green overlapping
         each other in 3 different mixtures. At the bottom, green is
         in front, at the top, blue dominates, and in the middle there is
         almost a middle mixture. Compare and differentiate
         the boundaries on both sides of each mixture.

XI-3   It will be immediately clear that of the 3 horizontal black bars
        which overlap and mix with the broad vertical white
        (in 3 different greys), the lower bar appears on top of the white,
        whereas the upper bar looks overlapped by the white and therefore
        behind or underneath it.
        Or, when following the white upward, it starts behind the black,
        but ends up on top of it.
        Such readings are caused by the dominating contents of the mixtures,
        as well as by their boundaries.
        The lower mixture obviously contains more black and the upper
        mixture, just as clearly, more white.

        Since the harder and therefore leading boundaries are
        products of the dominating stronger contents, they define the
        movement of the mixture.
        As a result, the harder, louder boundaries of the lower bar
        are horizontal, which means separation upward and downward, and
        moving sideward. The dominating boundaries of the upper, lighter
        mixture are vertical connections, sideward separations, and
        moving upward.
        Indirectly, this also explains the mixture in the middle.
        The black and white contents are equal, or nearly equal, and so
        are the mixture boundaries; all of which indicates that neither black
        nor white is on top, but that both penetrate each other on a
        2-dimensional level—without any spatial separation—and thus
        show a "middle mixture."

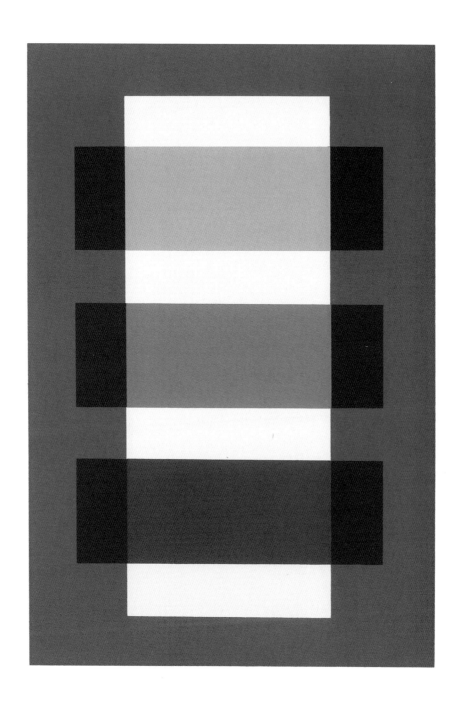

XI-3   This bright study is more or less self-explanatory.
        3 unconnected vertical bars of different deep colors are crossed
        by 3 separate horizontal bars of 1 and the same light color.

        Within their crossings appear 9 illusionary mixtures. The
        3 lower ones are dominated by the same light color and therefore
        appear on top of the darker verticals. The 3 upper mixtures
        are dominated by the 3 different deep colors which therefore
        appear on the top of the light color. In the middle horizontal
        bar, all colors meet on 1 and the same level.

        For a closer study, compare the 6 trios of mixtures. First,
        their similar increases and decreases within the horizontal bars;
        then, the gradual changes within the trios of the vertical bars.

        Be aware that any mixture is darker
        than the lighter of the mixture parents.

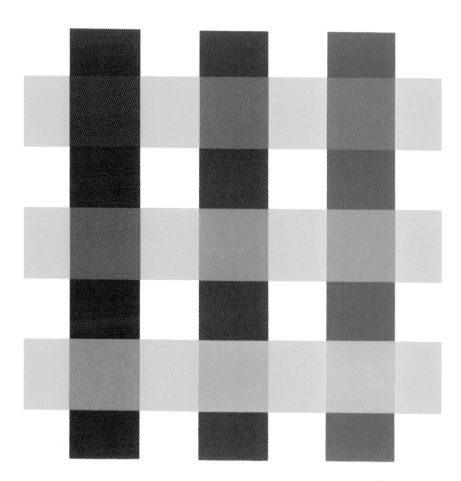

Optical mixture
CHAPTER XII

In contrast to after-image, here is another very different color illusion,
"optical mixture." 2 or more colors perceived simultaneously appear
combined as a third actual color, a mixture which annuls and replaces
the previous factual colors. (See Text, page 33.)

XII-2   Turn the page so that the white dots are at the right.
The size of the circular elements in blue, green, and white demands
observation from a distance. At right, compare the lightest whites
with the empty and filled whites, then with the smaller whites
at the left.
Looking from the left, compare all the blues—those with and without ground
in the middle, those with green and with white centers,
and those appearing as centers of green and white. In the middle
see and compare similarly the greens and their changes
through optical mixture.
See the whole also in a vertical position when more than
3 colors seem to appear in varying spatial positions.

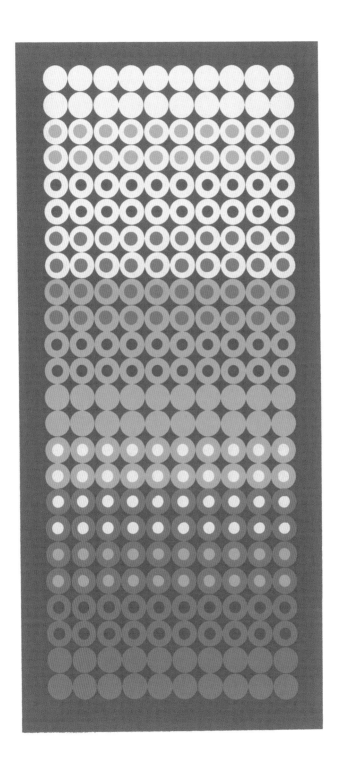

The Bezold Effect
CHAPTER XIII

XIII-1 The French Impressionists (after 1870) aimed at an optical mixture effect. Instead of mixing their colors on their palettes, they applied them in small dabs on the canvas so that the colors were mixed, at a distance, in our eyes.

A similar effect is named after Wilhelm von Bezold (1837–1907), a meteorologist in Berlin, who discovered that certain strong colors, when evenly distributed, changed entirely the effect of his rug designs, which were his avocation.*

One of my color students, following Bezold's example, showed in plate XIII-1 light red bricks laid up with very white mortar, and then showed the same bricks laid up with pure black mortar. The red with the white looks much lighter than the red with the black, particularly at a distance.

*The Theory of Color and Its Relation to Art and Art Industry, trans., Boston, Prang, 1876.

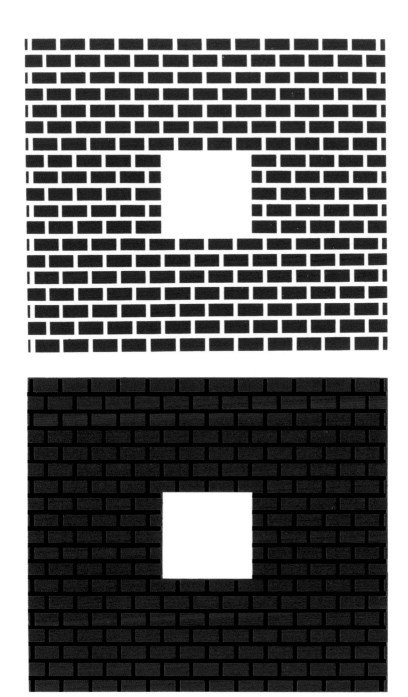

XIII-2 The change of 1 color alters both light and weight of
        the original, and, one can say, its speed and age as well.

        Another reading: besides the Bezold Effect, its opposite
        appears here—an after-image effect—when the dark red flanking
        the black is compared with the same red accompanying
        the white. Define this change.

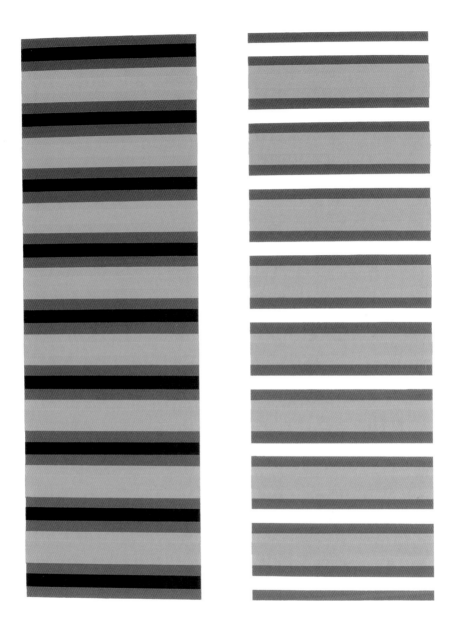

XIII-3   This commercial decorative design for a printed textile (of questionable merit) is
the point of departure for proving the Bezold Effect.
It shows the original condition in the upper part.

Substituting white for the black, it lights up
all other colors, which is the aim of the Bezold Effect
and of this study.

129

Color intervals and transformation
CHAPTER XIV

XIV-1   A "transformation" of 4 reds to 4 blues of a slightly lower key seems comparable to a transformation of a tetrachord in music from 1 instrument to another. Therefore we are also in color concerned with "intervals." But such rearrangement is far more complicated with colors than with musical notes.

Upstairs in plate XIV-1 we have 4 red squares at the left, making 1 square, and 4 blue squares at the right, also making a square. Each has its darkest squares on the left. In the top row of each the strongest contrast exists between the left and right squares, and they are separated by the hardest boundaries.

To demonstrate whether they provide the same "intervals," downstairs we transfer the blue square arrangement to the center of the reds, and vice versa. After this transformation, if the intervals are correct, the hardest boundary in the top pairs of squares is repeated in the upper halves of the vertical axis, and the lower pairs show the evenly softer boundaries.

In order to train your eyes, compare the corresponding boundaries upstairs and downstairs, from left to right. Then you will see that in all four cases the left vertical halves are heavier and that the right vertical halves are foggy. Read Chapter XIV and look at the 6 drawings that illustrate it.

XIV-2 Hold plate XIV-2 so that the 3 figures appear side by side.
A tetrachord of 4 juxtaposed reds (2 shades + 2 tints)
is presented in 3 equal repetitions. The 4 reds are then transformed
into 3 other hues—to 2 deeper keys of blue (left) and grey (center),
and to a higher key of orange (right).
For a comparison of the intervals of the 4 tones within all 4 hues,
the transformations are placed, in reduced size, in the centers
of the 3 repeated red juxtapositions, now serving as grounds
and thus as a common measure.
Although the blues may appear lighter than the surrounding reds,
they factually are all darker than the neighboring reds
in diffused daylight (indoors and outdoors), in full sunlight,
and also in warm and in cool artificial light.

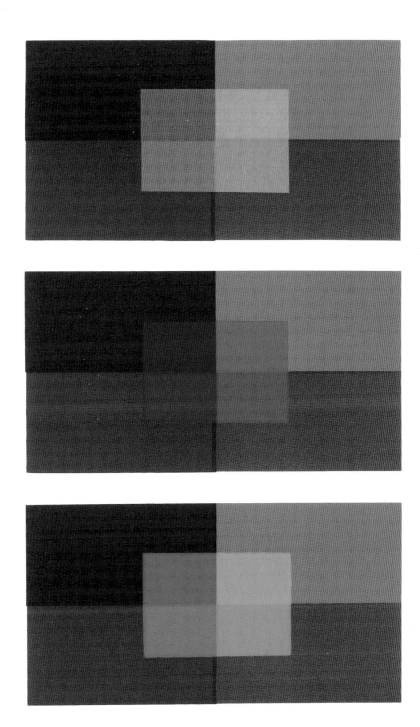

XIV-3   Here, 4 colors different in hue and in light are changed into
         4 other colors equally different but of a higher key. Both tetrachords
         then exchanged present a convincing as well as pleasing
         transformation. Both are united by the lightweight left halves
         and by the fuller right halves.

Intersection
CHAPTER XV

xv-1   Hold plates xv-1 so that the yellow and green rectangles are on the left.
Cut off the flap so that you have a separate sheet that is printed on both sides,
with single and double dots keying the proper color to each study.
This sheet we place so close to the right boundary of the first color
at the left that only a small strip of the second color (about ¼" wide)
remains visible.
While staring at this small strip, move the loose sheet
slowly to the right, and thus reveal more and more of the
second color, the central color. When this is done a new illusion occurs:
The central color looks more and more like 2 colors, repeating
at the left boundary the color of the right neighbor, at the right the color
of the left neighbor.
This study works best in incandescent (warm) artificial light.
To accustom oneself to the phenomenon,
the exercise should be shown repeatedly.

XV-1

XV-2 Turn the page so that the bright pink rectangle is at the left.
When staring at the center of the study, immediately
the central color will appear as 2 colors, repeating
at the left contour the color of the field at right, and at the
right contour the neighboring color at the left. It looks as if
each of the outer colors were moving underneath the middle color
and turning up at the other end—penetrating, or, better, intersecting
each other very softly.
(To demonstrate this in 3 dimensions, intersect the straight fingers
of both hands, and look at them from above. Then, palms of the hands up,
intersect the straight fingers again. This illustrates intersection
even better.)

This new kind of transparence proves a new measure for such mixtures.
After some observation it becomes obvious whether the mixture contains
equal or unequal amounts of the 2 mixture parents.
Here the central field looks evenly mixed in daylight and under
warm plus cool fluorescent light. But under warm incandescent light,
especially at some distance, the pink dominates by far
the smaller amount of brown.

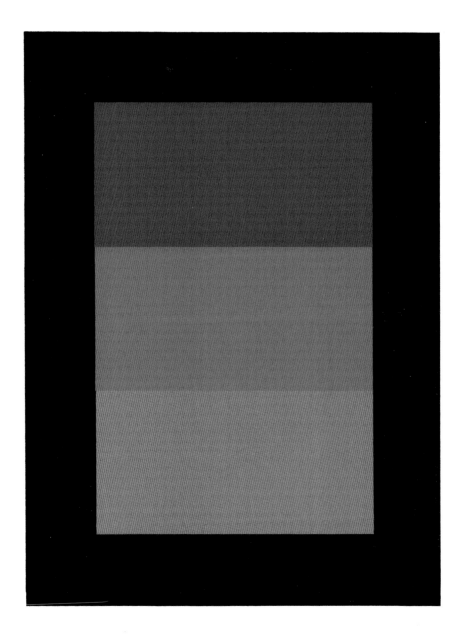

XV-2   To achieve a new sculptural illusion of intersecting colors, note
that the separating boundaries of a middle mixture look elevated,
or raised from the ground, which causes a "fluting" effect
known from the channelings of a Doric column.

Here is a "blown up" view of the fluting effect: Consider the dark red rectangle
as a ground plan, and read the channelings as 2 side elevations.

Quantity
CHAPTER XVI

This is a new kind of exercise, exploring how changes of quantity in color
can change appearance and influence of color.

XVI-1   View all 4 studies simultaneously, so that the stripes appear vertical.
They show a first approach to a solution of the problem (described on
page 43 of the Text). Here the 4 grounds are the largest areas
occupied alternatingly by each of the 4 colors.
Each color then carries the 3 other colors as figure,
in stripes of very different placements, and each, through connection
or separation, appears in wide or narrow, loose or tight groupings.

Although the pink appears somewhat dominant (which can be justified),
the 4 panels are of 4 different characters.
This will be more obvious when we look at them as walls,
much wider than high, by covering (simplest by hand)
the upper two-thirds of each panel. First, consider yourself
confronting each wall, and then, seeing others against these walls.

XVI-1

XVI-1

XVI-2   This is a stimulus for further variants. Look at them not
as 1 group, but in series, rows, or smaller groups
by blocking them out (with slip sheet or hands), and look at
particular single studies through adjusted openings.

Select your favorite studies, and find the reason for your preference
(but also for your rejections). And learn that your preferences
won't be constant, but will change with time and your own conditions,
just as prejudices do.

See that such systematic studies go beyond self-expression
and avoid self-disclosure. Instead, they lead us to comparison,
and so to evaluation, and further to self-criticism
and self-education.

Please do not ask which is the "best" design,
although we have seen this question printed, because,
without further qualification as to cause and purpose,
this question is both unjustified and irrelevant.
It merely discloses the incompetence of the inquirer.
(See comments on variants and variety, page 73 of the Text.)

XVI-3 An unusual solution. Besides its representation in 4 circles
        and its subordination under a severe restriction—that is,
        a precisely repeated subdivision of the 4 circles—it demonstrates
        clearly the extreme cases of connection and separation within and
        among circles: The inner centrifugal enclosure
        —cohesion—against the outer centrifugal enclosure
        —adhesion.

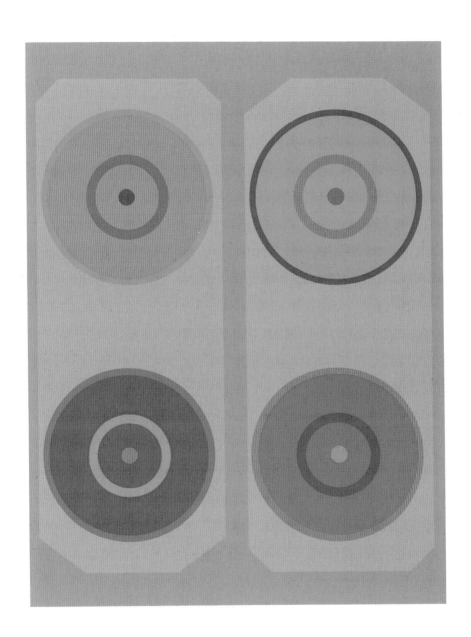

XVI-3　A most successful "quantity study," and an amazing
　　　　reversal of the initial inclination to employ
　　　　the ground as the largest area. Here, the figure above the ground
　　　　dominates through recurrence plus amount, or repetition
　　　　plus extension.

Film and volume color

XVII-1   (b.) Over 4 tints a shadow is cast, through transformation
          into a lower key.
          (t.) By reversing the lower study, a light is cast,
          as in a transformation study into a higher key.
          If the lightening up appears the same for all shades,
          it proves that the solution at the bottom is correct.

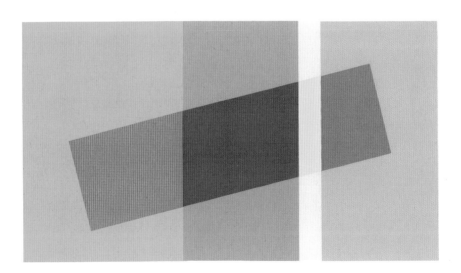

XVII-1   An illusion of film color indicating a sheet of almost
          clear acetate covering 4 colors, and at right
          covering even twice. But remember that the
          original study is done not in transparent material
          but in opaque paper, which, of course, demands a
          very precise color selection.

XVII-2 A study in opaque paper demonstrating an illusion
of transparence in film color.
This reminds us of varnish applied first on 3 of 5
stripes in 4 colors, then over 5 stripes.
Count the number of colors necessary to make
this study or a reproduction in paper or in ink.

Free studies
CHAPTER XVIII

These studies are to prove that a systematic step-by-step learning
through obligatory class problems does not handicap personal development.
The repeatedly expressed expectation that a concentration on obligatory
class problems disturbs individual talents and interests
has been proved wrong.

As correct grammar and proper spelling must not obstruct poetic creation,
so clear observation and clean articulation must not lead to a domineering
school fashion or style,
nor to an obedient and imitative discipleship.

These free studies offer a study of differences: differences in attitude,
procedure, and aim; differences as to affinity and contrast of means;
and differences in their application. They invite one to distinguish remaining
or changing tempo, pace, and speed; topographic directions, such as in and out,
lateral, vertical, or centered motion;
effects achieved, avoided, and overlooked. And so on.

XVIII–1   An interesting activation is demonstrated here. Whereas
a strictly repeated pattern never is read through—
from beginning to end, that is—here a continued modification
produces a near-pattern design inviting us to a
comprehensive "looking through."

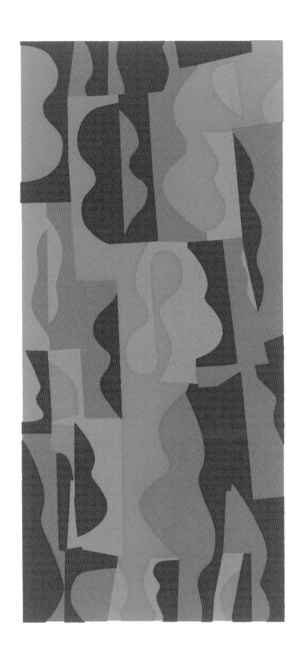

XVIII-2 In our color course we do not teach composition or related rules
to be followed or applied. We also avoid speaking of "color
design" in pictorial use of color.

We prefer to make comparisons between pictorial organization
and cooking, for instance, because of its measuring of amount
and flavor and its continuous tasting. Or we find parallels
with conducting, because of its coordination of emphasis and
subordination, and because of its rehearsing before performance.
In our free studies we aim at a visually challenging
interplay of influencing and influenced colors—in other words,
a presentation of active relatedness.

Here 1 distinctive shape dominates. Many circles of equal size
are tightly connected in horizontal-vertical rows.
Thus they present a mechanical and easy distribution,
extending over the entire space, leaving in-between spaces
of only 1 shape and size.
The only freedom left, it seems, is a choice of color and light.
We recommend such organization of "restricted means,"
because a limitation in 1 direction often opens more
freedom in other directions.
For another restriction (not in form, as here), we suggest
"a restricted palette"—a limitation to a few colors,
or to 1 hue only, to 2-voiced instead of multi-voiced, and especially
to monochromatic juxtaposition.

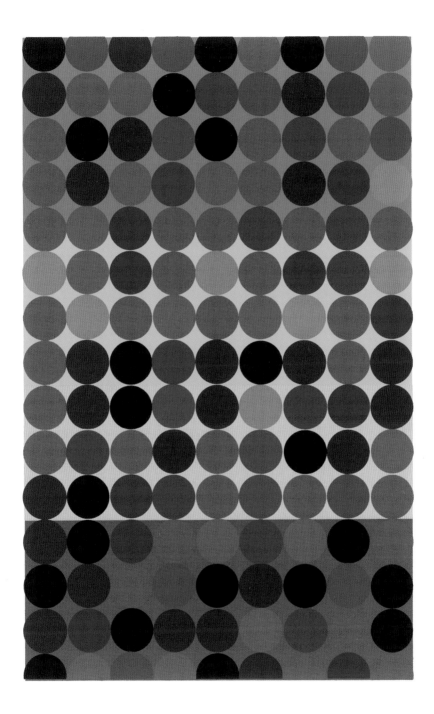

XVIII-3 A typical but successful assemblage in color paper. Quite free
         of color harmony, each color manages to "save its own face."
         Although loosely lined up, through a distinct relationship of
         the outer shapes and the inner features, it is held in a firm unity
         and an equilibrium of independence and
         dependence.

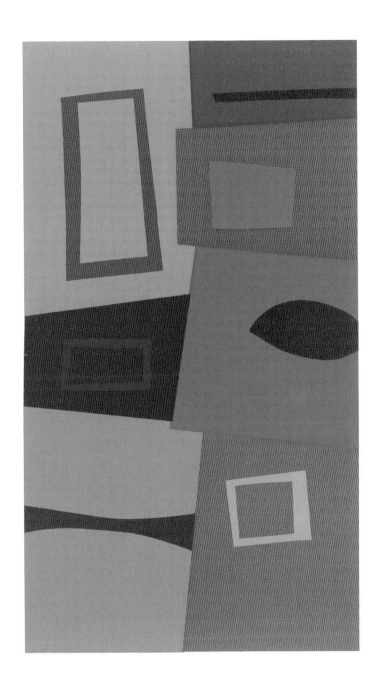

XVIII-3 A double interaction between 2 dimmed tones of red and green
combines 2 contrasting effects, an after-image with its opposite,
an optical mixture.
Whereas the more frequent and even subdivision
of the outer areas tends toward a greyed-down optical mixture,
the after-image occurs in the elliptical center, where
the green ground—after a figure-ground exchange—shows
a larger broadening than the reds.
The numerical reduction of stripes in the center consequently
produces a clear increase in both light and color for the green,
but a gain only in color, with a loss in light, for the red.
All of this results in a subtle change in posture,
from an outer soft flatness to a central emphasis of direction.
And both are reversed by a strong figure-ground change
through the horizontal center line.

XVIII-9 An arrangement of stripes of very contrasting character.
These can be read (from bottom to top) first, as warm and soft
against hard and cool; second, with relation to interiors,
as a heavy carpet against a light papered wall; and third,
if considered as sounds, as woodwinds against brass.

In addition, there is a harmonious and sonorous assemblage
of adjacent colors which makes the blues look warm.
All these differences can be read
despite the fact that all the colors appear in the shape
of stripes, stripes which are all equally
"hard-edged."

XVIII-11   Once or twice during a color course we limit the independence we have
                for free studies. Then, in order to get closely related studies
                which invite an intensified comparison, the whole class submits
                to a given combination of 3 or 4 colors in paper. They are
                selected by students or teachers, or are chosen as a restricted palette
                from a challenging study by a class member.

                Such studies of equal instrumentation not only will remind us
                of our inclinations and aversions for certain colors, but will
                help to clarify where and when our choice and neglect appear
                justified and when not.

                Notice that this study includes
                the white of the ground as active color.

The Masters
CHAPTER XIX

XIX-1   (l.) This study is not a copy in the usual understanding of a replica.
(See Text, page 53.) As Van Gogh copied Daumier, for instance,
and Cézanne copied Italian masters, in a free personal manner and mainly
to clarify one or another particular viewpoint, so this transformation
into color paper is not a repetitious duplication. It purposely neglects
many details and even may appear in changed keys of light and temperature.
It is a consciously condensed record of a personal notation
of a painting's color instrumentation, or, in usual terms,
of its palette and color relatedness.

(r.) The unavoidable flattening of the 4-color process with its loss of opacity
and plasticity of the paints in the original unfortunately
shows its leveling effects here, by losing the directness,
freshness, and solidity of the pasted paper colors
and their tactile edges.

It should be easy to distinguish here the study in paper from its
"reproduced original." This study is based on a work by Matisse.

The Weber-Fechner Law
CHAPTER XX

XX-1 4 equal rectangles of the same color,
a translucent yellow, overlap each other in a systematic order which
produces 4 different yellows separated by 3 different kinds
of boundaries.

Only the central square consists of 4 layers of yellow.
Surrounding it there are 4 squares consisting of 3 layers,
then 8 shapes of 2 layers, and around them all—8 shapes of 1 layer only.

For a precise recognition, locate each group of squares singly.

For a reading in an opposite direction, differentiate:
all outer shapes show only 1 layer of yellow, therefore are lightest.
These 8 shapes, through continued corner connections, present 8 pairs.
Each pair surrounds, alternatingly with 2 or 3 edges,
1 double, 5 single, and 1 quarter square, all of 2 layers of yellow
which naturally are darker than 1 layer of yellow.

Similarly, all shapes of 2 layers are connected again as a ring
—to 8 pairs—or to 4 trios—embracing 4 squares of 3 layers of yellow.
These latter 4 squares of 3 layers
enclose entirely (through both corner and edge connections)
the center square which alone has 4 layers, and therefore is darkest,
and has the softest, almost vanishing boundaries.

This heaping of translucent yellow on white paper in 1 to 4 layers
presents (physically) gradual mixtures in an arithmetical progression.
But in our perception the gradual reduction of light within the yellows,
as well as the gradual softening of the boundaries between them,
is of a geometric proportion.

Both reductions—or increases, when read the opposite way—
demonstrate the Weber-Fechner Law (see Text, page 54).

It is easy to conclude that an additional fifth layer
would hardly increase the darkening of the yellow,
nor would it mark further boundary separation.

XX-1　2 gradation scales for a comparison of arithmetical and
geometric progression in mixture of color (here red and black).
Both are to be read downward, thus beginning with red.

(l.) To the upper red is mixed successively 1 - 2 - 3 - 4
equal amounts of black, as has been recommended by
M. E. Chevreul (see Text, page 54) and which presents
an arithmetical progression, but only physically,
not perceptually.
(r.) To the same red is added successively 1 - 2 - 4 - 8
equal measures of black, thus presenting a geometric progression—
following the Weber-Fechner Law.

(l. & r.) Both gradations are alike within the first 2 steps.
And both have the same psychological or perceptual aim—
an arithmetical progression. But the results are different:
At left a diminishing increase of black;
at right a steady increase of black.
The difference shows still more clearly at a distance.

As we learned with illusional transparence, the pronunciation of
boundaries measures spatial relationship. Consequently, all the steps
at the right, including the last one, are separated by equally clear edges,
which give them equal height. At the left the steps merge
visually more and more as we look downward, and
the last separation is least recognizable.
Both results prove the Weber-Fechner Law—indirectly at left,
and directly at right.

After producing such scales in pasted layers of
very lightly colored acetate sheets, accompany them
with linear diagrams, showing in steps, or in
continuous lines, (a) the physical content and
(b) the psychological effect of both scales.

Warm-cool
CHAPTER XXI

XXI-1 Red and blue, usually representing warm and cool,
are placed alternately on the left and right sides
to demonstrate that both colors can look high as well as
low in temperature. Such a placement will easily provoke
disagreement. But a reading of all the left halves
warmer than the paired right halves is not unreasonable.

Vibrating boundaries
CHAPTER XXII

XXII-1 2 contrasting or near-contrasting colors are arranged
to produce an effect of vibrating boundaries (see Text, page 61).
In case you wear glasses, look at the studies with and without them,
and, if possible, in near and far focus.
Distinguish also where the doubling of the contour occurs,
outside or inside of the figures.
Observe them also in daylight and in different artificial lights.

Notice that these studies are done in regular color paper,
not in so-called "day-glow" paper. Whereas the effect of the
latter depends on a new kind of fluorescent pigment,
here the vibration effect appears
as an illusion for which we have no known explanation.

XXII-2   Turn the page so the green center square is on the left.
2 studies of precisely the same arrangement,
but with reversed colors. That the vibrating
boundaries look different on both sides is probably the result
of the changing color quantities of figure and ground.

For another reading of such illusionary vibration, one can
recall auras and halos.

Equal light intensity
CHAPTER XXIII

XXIII-1   2 tints, ochre and pink, are purposely shown
in aggressive shapes, indicating 2 two-edged saws.
At left they are separated, except for point connections.
But when fully connected, as at right, and when seen
at some distance, the 10 sharp teeth, clearly marked
at left, almost disappear in a smooth merging of the
2 different colors. The reason for this loss of form
is the equal or near-equal light intensity of the 2 colors.
(See Text, page 62.)

XXIII-2 Here is a figure extending sideward and
with many sharp corners. Although all shapes
are similar triangles, clearly constructed—with pointed
corners and straight lines—we cannot be sure in the top figure
whether we see, at a short distance, several figures or only 1.
And it is not possible to count all the triangles, much less
their corners. The contours vanish because the 2 colors
are of the same light intensity.
Only when the triangles are seen against a white
background is it revealed that there are in fact
11 triangles with 21 corners.

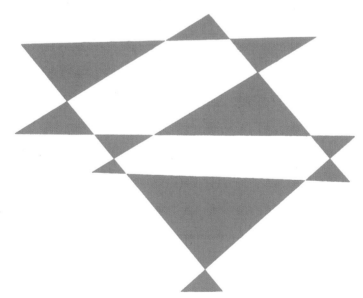

Color theories
CHAPTER XXIV

XXIV-1 The Equilateral Triangle

It is probably the most condensed and clear system of presentation of
an essential order in the vast world of color.
Within the 2 dimensions of an equilateral triangle—subdivided
in 9 similar triangles—are 3 primaries, 3 secondaries, and
(unexpectedly) 3 tertiaries, all placed very sensibly.

The first of the 3 trios, containing the strongest color contrasts,
appears most separated, at the extreme ends—in the 3 corners.
Yellow and blue (which Goethe called "the only 2 pure colors," and
also "the primeval contrast") appropriately hold the base.
And red ("the middle between them") occurs high off at the apex,
again separated but in a middle place.
The less opposite secondaries are in the middle of the
outer edges, and the closest, or least different, tertiaries
naturally meet still more in the center.

The drawings on page 66 of the Text show 3 more groupings
which invite further study of relationships within the groups
 and also among the groups.
We suggest copying the 9 groupings on tracing paper
(on top of the equilateral triangle) and cutting
them as stencils for further comparisons.

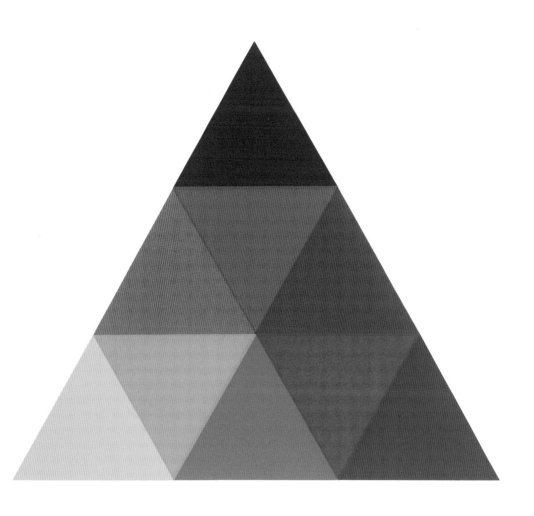

Leaf studies

XXV-2
&
XXV-6 The studies of pressed fall leaves and color paper do not need detailed description.
Notice how different they are, and see them as independent work
of students trained in basic class exercises which aim first
at single color effects only, and thus train for the development
of active color relationship—by practical realization of
color interaction.
Recognize the manifold use of the material, the changing organization
and presentation—unhampered by either harmony or disharmony,
but led by respect for both—discord and concord.

XXV-2

XXV-6

Josef Albers, one of the most influential artist-educators of the twentieth century, was a member of the Bauhaus in Germany during the 1920s. In 1933 he came to the United States, where he taught at Black Mountain College for sixteen years. In 1950 he joined the faculty at Yale University as chairman of the Department of Design; after his retirement in 1958 he was named emeritus professor of art, a position he held until his death in 1976. The recipient of numerous awards and honorary degrees, Albers was elected to the National Institute of Arts and Letters in 1968 and in 1971 was the first living artist ever to be given a solo retrospective at The Metropolitan Museum of Art in New York.

Nicholas Fox Weber is executive director of the Josef and Anni Albers Foundation.